ENTERTAINING ANGELS
Hospitality Programs for the Caring Church

"*Entertaining Angels* will challenge you to look anew at your assumptions regarding the role of hospitality, evangelism, and outreach in today's church. . . . This book begins where others leave off. This book delivers."

> The Rt. Rev. G.P. Mellick Belshaw
> Bishop of New Jersey

"This is *not* a guide on how to increase numbers on the parish rolls, although numerical growth will almost automatically result from following even a few of the suggestions the author presents. First and foremost, however, it is about the theology of ministry to newcomers. It is as much about the *why* of hospitality as the *how*."

> The Rev. Dr. Margaret Guenther, Director
> The Center for Christian Spirituality
> *author of* Holy Listening: The Art of Spiritual Direction

"Here is a how-to resource that is much needed. . . . The author weaves together the church–business connection through biblical insights, sound scholarship, personal experience, and practical suggestions for parish programming. Every business person seeking to make the connection between their faith and their work can benefit from her insight and creative suggestions in her chapter, 'Outreach to the Business Community.' "

> John G. Heimann, Chairman
> Global Financial Institutions Group
> Merrill Lynch

"Elizabeth Geitz has written a buoyant book about our ministry as guests and hosts. Building on root metaphors of hospitality found in the Scriptures and drawing upon her own experience of parish life, she has produced an eminently practical guide to the mysterious art of welcoming strangers to the glory of God."

> John T. Koenig
> Sub-Dean, General T̶ ̶ ̶ ̶
> autho̶ ̶ ̶ ̶
> and ̶

ENTERTAINING ANGELS
Hospitality Programs for the Caring Church

Elizabeth Rankin Geitz

MOREHOUSE PUBLISHING
Harrisburg, PA

Morehouse Publishing
P.O. Box 1321
Harrisburg, PA 17105

Library of Congress Cataloging-in-Publication Data
Geitz, Elizabeth Rankin.
        Entertaining angels : hospitality programs for the caring church / Elizabeth
Rankin Geitz.
        p.   cm.
        Includes bibliographical references.
        ISBN 0-8192-1601-1 (paper)
        1. Hospitality—Religious aspects—Christianity.   2. Church work with new
church members.   I. Title.
BV4647.H67G45   1993   92-45259
259—dc20   CIP

Second Printing, 1994

Printed in the United States of America

"Let mutual love continue. Do not neglect to show hospitality to strangers, for by doing that some have entertained angels without knowing it." (Hebrews 13:1-2)

For Michael, my husband,

and for Charlotte and Michael R., my children,

God's gifts of abundant love to me

TABLE OF CONTENTS

ACKNOWLEDGMENTS

Grateful acknowledgment is made to the following publishers and individuals for permission to use the works cited:

To Abingdon Press for permission to print an excerpt from Howard Miller's *How to Build a Magnetic Church*, © 1987, page 63.

To the Crossroad Publishing Company for permission to reprint "A Psalm About Grieving" and a prayer for those who grieve, from *WOMANWISDOM: A Feminist Lectionary and Psalter— Women of the Hebrew Scriptures, Part One* by Miriam Therese Winter, pages 250 and 251, © 1991 by Medical Mission Sisters.

To the William Morris Agency for permission to adapt an excerpt from the Introduction to *The Listener*, © 1960 by Taylor Caldwell.

To the Rev. William Heuss for permission to reprint "The Last Pew" from *The Episcopal Times*, Boston, Diocese of Massachusetts.

To the Rev. Christopher Chamberlin Moore for permission to reprint "Hello, I am a Newcomer to Your Church."

To William Morrow and Company Inc. for permission to print an excerpt from *Behind the Scenes*, by Michael K. Deaver with Mickey Herskowitz, © 1988 by Michael K. Deaver.

To the family of Mary Sammons Patton for permission to reprint "Lines to Starlings on a Snowy Day" and "To a Bulb" from *Hearts Birds Freed*, © 1992, pages 98-99 and 13.

To Patrick Powers for permission to reprint the title song from his play, *Angels*.

To the United Methodist Publishing House for permission to reprint two prayers from *The Book of Services*, © 1985, pages 83 and 90.

To David McKay Co., Inc., a subsidiary of Random House, for permission to adapt material from pages 42-44 and 47-48 of *Parent Effectiveness Training*, © 1970 by Thomas Gordon.

"... FOR GOD ALL THINGS ARE POSSIBLE."
(Matthew 19:26, Mark 10:27)

This book could never have been written without the hospitality of the many angels God has sent my way. At just the right moment, someone would suddenly appear to offer insight and encouragement to this pilgrim along her journey of researching, writing, and editing. As I prayed for God's guidance throughout the process, my prayers were indeed answered by many, who have taught me much about hospitality and the offering of one's gifts to the other.

My heartfelt appreciation goes first of all to my family, my husband Michael and my children, Charlotte and Michael R., who have graciously given me the gift of time to spend endless hours at my word processor, especially on those beautiful summer days when that was the last place they wanted me to be. None of this would have been possible without their encouragement, patience and support. Many thanks also go to Anne Harris, whose commitment to me and to my family throughout this process is deeply appreciated.

In addition, without the insightful and caring comments of many, this book would be far less than it is. My gratitude is extended to the Rev. Dr. John Koenig, the Rev. Leslie Smith, the Rev. A.Wayne Schwab, the Rev. Professor J. Neil Alexander, the Rev. Michael Allen, the Rev. Lisa Lancaster, the Rev. Professor Daniel Hardy, Sister Lorette Piper, Michael Geitz, Aline Haynes, Leslie Hawke, David Prescott, Charlotte Taylor, and Barbara Barnett for their superb suggestions on content, after reading portions of the original manuscript. My appreciation also goes to the Rt. Rev. G.P. Mellick Belshaw, the Rev. Christopher C. Moore and the Episcopal Diocese of New Jersey for their enthusiastic commitment to the original booklet,

Welcoming the Stranger, which gave birth to this book.

I offer further thanks to a special angel God sent my way who does not even know me; the Reverend Harrison Simons, who on his own, mailed *Welcoming the Stranger* to Morehouse Publishing, suggesting that they publish the work. Many thanks also go to Deborah Grahame-Smith, my editor at Morehouse, whose sincere interest in this book and all that is in it has provided me with much encouragement throughout the editing and rewriting process.

Finally, I thank my father, Oscar L. Rankin, and the memory of my mother, Dorothy B. Rankin, for encouraging me always to be all that God created me to be. I also thank my brothers, Lane and Bradley, two of my greatest supporters, both now and in the past.

INTRODUCTION

One winter day in 1983, the Very Rev. Richard A. Bower stopped me in the halls of Trinity Church, Princeton, New Jersey, and asked, "Elizabeth, do you think you could chair our Newcomer Committee this year?" Since I was involved in numerous other church activities, I hesitated. "With all my other commitments, I just don't see how I can possibly add one more," I replied. "Well, why don't you pray about it?" he asked.

At that moment, I knew what my answer would be, for I knew firsthand of the need in a large church for a structured newcomer program. As my husband and I looked for a church home, following our move to New Jersey from South Carolina, there was an immediately apparent difference between churches. Some were friendly and welcoming. Some were not. Some followed up on our visit. Some did not. What was the difference? I discovered that very few churches had a structured newcomer committee at that time. All churches wanted to be welcoming. All wanted to attract new members. Yet few had a specific newcomer program to enable that to occur.

Why might this be so? T.S. Eliot wrote, "Between the idea/ and the reality/Between the motion/And the act,/Falls the Shadow." As Trinity's Newcomer chairperson, I soon discovered that between the idea and the reality of establishing a parish-wide newcomer program falls the shadow of time. Countless hours are needed, not only to read available material but also to develop the necessary forms, to set up a working committee, and to train those who have chosen this ministry.

I searched for resources to help me with the nuts-and-bolts aspects of newcomer ministry. But my search was in vain, so I began the arduous task of developing the material on my own.

13

Several years later I wrote my first newcomer article for the Alban Institute's *Action Information* and, along with it, offered a Newcomer Kit with all the forms needed to set up a church program. To my surprise, I began receiving orders and notes of thanks from churches of all denominations throughout the United States and Canada. There seemed to be a real need for practical, how-to information on setting up newcomer systems.

Then I took the next step of developing a workshop to train laity to develop and run their own newcomer programs. After giving this workshop in churches across the state, I was urged to put all the material together for publication and distribution. *Welcoming the Stranger* was then published in hopes of illuminating the shadow of which T.S. Eliot wrote, with the light of a simple how-to newcomer program, complete with both the forms to implement it and a workshop with handouts to introduce it. This material, updated and significantly expanded, became what is now Chapters 3, 4, and 5 of this book. But still something was missing. What was it?

After beginning my seminary education at Princeton Theological Seminary and continuing at General Theological Seminary, I realized what was missing. No newcomer ministry book I had ever seen, including my own, gave a thorough examination of the theological and biblical basis for establishing such a program. I became convinced that what churches are offering is newcomer *ministry*, rather than merely a newcomer program. Thus, laity needed to be educated in why it is a ministry. Why do we as Christian people extend hospitality to the stranger? How are we as a church different from community organizations in our welcoming? In addressing these questions, Chapters 1 and 2 were created.

At this point, I thought I had written a book that included most of what a church would need to know about newcomer or hospitality ministry. But I am now convinced that God had other ideas in mind. For God kept presenting me with opportunities to develop other types of parish programs. For several years I had no idea that these particular programs were in any way connected to my involvement in newcomer ministry. My work with the poor in an inner-city area, with the bereaved, and with newcomers seemed unrelated, except that all involved ministering in the name of Christ. It gradually dawned on me that I was wrong. There was a connection—a powerful connection. As these programs were put in place, I observed that through them, new people were attracted to the church. This was hospitality outreach through parish programming. I had never conceived of such a possibility, yet here it was happening before my eyes. Thus, Chapter 6 was born.

I thought the book was complete, but God had still more for me to see, through other interesting revelations. At the same time I was working in the inner city, I was also attending elegant business functions with my husband in New York City, related to his job. I was certain that this had nothing to do with ministry. For me, it had more to do with feeling guilty about the money that was being spent on such events. Wrong again. For over a period of years, God opened my eyes to even more possibilities. After much thought and prayer, I realized that God was presenting me with yet another opportunity to reach out and bring others into the body of Christ. I then began to research systematic ways this might be accomplished within a business environment—and Chapter 7 came into being.

This book, which is the compilation of ten years of work, reflection, study, and prayer, is offered in thanksgiving for the many opportunities God has given me for ministry. It is also offered, with my blessings, to all who hear the still, small voice of God calling them to a ministry of hospitality.

Elizabeth

PART I

Chapter 1

BIBLICAL PERSPECTIVES
ON HOSPITALITY

At different times in our lives, each of us has been the stranger. As God creates us anew, challenging us, calling us, leading us, we may at times feel like a stranger to ourselves. We may marvel at the person we are becoming, as we search to understand just who that person is. As we grow through God's love for us, we can also feel like a stranger in relation to those we love most and know best. These times call us into new relationships based on sharing, mutuality, and reaching out one to the other.

As children, when we first enter kindergarten or first grade, we are indeed the stranger—to new surroundings, new people, and new expectations. Later, as adults, we often find ourselves in the role of stranger—in college, in the workplace, in evolving relationships, in new communities. Thus, being the stranger is fundamental to the human experience. Simply being, living, moving, through the life cycle, we will at times find ourselves strangers in an alien land—confused, seeking, and hoping for a comforting word of reassurance.

Perhaps it is for this reason that we often find in the story of God's people, our story. For our Hebrew mothers and fathers were indeed strangers in an alien land. Their physical journey from bondage in Egypt, through the wilderness, toward the promised land, parallels our own life journey—a journey with twists and unexpected turns, a journey with numerous wilderness experiences, a journey on which we are all both guests and hosts.

As we as Christian people look seriously at welcoming the stranger into our faith communities, it is critical that we connect with the experience of our Judeo-Christian forebears. Where does our story intersect with theirs? What role did hospitality play in their lives? Without such an understanding of the scriptural and theological basis for extending hospitality to the stranger, we run the risk of becoming merely another community Welcome Wagon, bringing others into our fellowship so they can begin to feel at home in new surroundings; or we may incorrectly focus on church growth in terms of new members on the rolls or new pledges on the books.

What is it that marks the role of hospitality in the life of the Christian as distinct? To answer this question we must look not only at the lives of Jesus and Paul, but at the ethos of hospitality into which they, as Jews, were born.

Hospitality in the Judeo-Christian Tradition

Within first-century Judaism, Abraham was heralded as the supreme practitioner of hospitality. In Genesis 18:1–15, Abraham reached out in hospitality to three heavenly strangers, offering them a meal of curds, milk, calf meat and cakes. While they were eating, one gave him the seemingly impossible news that Sarah would bear a son in her old age. A few years prior to Jesus' ministry, a large monument was erected by Herod the Great on the supposed site of this meeting, not only commemorating the event, but highlighting its centrality within the Jewish tradition.[1]

In his book New Testament Hospitality John Koenig states: "Undergirding the great importance attached to openness toward guests was a hope shared by many first-century Jews that God would act as bountiful host at the end of time by entertaining Israel at an endless feast."[2] Therefore, first-century Jews hoped that by welcoming the stranger themselves, God would receive them into the kingdom just as hospitably. Likewise, if they did not receive the stranger warmly, they would be received in the same way at the end of time.

This belief gives us much to consider today. What if God receives us in the same way we have received those God sends to us? At the Great Coffee Hour in the Sky will we be sitting on the side, feeling left out and alone? Or will we be welcomed with open arms by those who are already comfortably in? Will they make room for us, or not really notice that we are there? As I think of the times I have left the role of welcomer to someone else, absorbed in my own comfortable conversations, this image gives me pause to reflect.

Hospitality to the stranger was not only central to first-century Jewish and Christian belief; both religions were dependent on such hospitality for their very existence. Knowledge of the Jewish faith was perpetuated and shared by traveling pairs of Jewish teachers. These itinerant teachers, of little material means, were dependent on the hospitality of those who welcomed them into their homes. In exchange for food and lodging, they shared their Torah wisdom with the family, their relatives, and their friends.[3]

Jesus, a first-century Jewish teacher himself, conformed to this tradition as he went about proclaiming the word of God. He was often invited into people's homes to share his wisdom at table fellowship.[4] While he was dining at the home of Simon the leper, a woman broke into the room and anointed Jesus' head with oil, a ritual reserved for messianic rulers. When she was rebuked by the guests, Jesus used the incident as a teaching tool. Mark 14:3–9 tells us that he not only affirmed the appropriateness of her action, but also stated that "wherever the good news is proclaimed in the whole world, what she has done will be told in remembrance of her. . . ." In another version of this story recorded by Luke, Jesus used the incident to teach the guests through a parable about forgiveness (Lk 7:36–50). Later, on his way to Jerusalem, Jesus "entered a certain village, where a woman named Martha welcomed him into her home" (Lk 10:38). As Martha prepared the meal, her sister Mary sat at Jesus' feet drinking in his wisdom. In numerous other homes throughout his ministry Jesus was welcomed and fed, even as he taught.

The spreading of the teachings of Jesus was indeed dependent on the hospitality of others. As he was welcomed, fed, and nourished after his day's journey, the seeds of the church were planted. The very foundations of our Christian faith were built on those who welcomed the stranger Jesus into their homes and hearts.

Similarly, as Paul traveled about, much of his teaching was done in homes. Like the Jewish rabbis and Jesus before him, he was often dependent on the hospitality of others for providing him a place to teach the word of God. As hospitality was extended, the good news was proclaimed. Without such welcoming, the gospel message may never have spread beyond the boundaries of Palestine.

Thus, the roots of hospitality within the Judeo-Christian tradition are deep and solid, reaching back to our forebears Sarah

and Abraham and spreading out to embrace those early teachers
of our faith upon whom the very existence of Christianity is dependent. Over the centuries, this hospitality has been offered
again and again in the name of Christ.

In my great-grandfather's autobiography, he tells of a
Southern religious revival held in 1879 where strangers were
welcomed, much as they were in Palestine, with kindness, food,
and lodging. "The chief vehicle of interest and attention for the
summer was the big meeting, held frequently under a brush
arbor. Literally thousands of people came, came with every mode
of conveyance. Every class and condition of people were repre-
sented. The utmost courtesy, good will and neighborliness pre-
vailed. Any stranger that wanted to attend the meeting could
get all he wanted to eat, a place to sleep and the kindest of treat-
ment."[5] Not only was hospitality extended in this nineteenth-
century meeting, but it was extended to "every class and
condition of people."

As we discuss welcoming the stranger into our faith communities today, we need to address the question, Who is the
stranger? Will every class and condition of people be equally
welcome in our churches? Who was the stranger in Jesus' day,
and who is the stranger for us now? In defining the stranger, we
can begin to define our role in welcoming those persons sent to
us by God.

Hospitality to All Strangers

In the movie *Sister Act*, its star Whoopi Goldberg, a raucous
nightclub singer and mistress in Reno, witnesses a murder. As a
result, her own life is in danger. For protection, the police decide
she should live in a convent, a most unlikely hideout. She is
taken to St. Katherine's Convent in San Francisco and directed
to the Mother Superior's study. Before the Mother Superior en-
ters, a monsignor informs her of Whoopi's predicament. The
Mother Superior agrees to accept Whoopi as a member of the
convent, until she opens the door and sees her. There sits
Whoopi, wearing a gold lamé coat, a purple-sequined outfit, and
a profusion of jewelry. The Mother Superior gasps and shuts the
door. The monsignor reminds her, in not-so-gentle tones, "You
have taken a vow of hospitality to all in need." With a straight
face, the Mother Superior replies, "I lied."

How often do we, upon seeing the strangers who come our way, say somewhere in our heart of hearts, "I lied—I lied when I took my baptismal vows and promised to seek and serve Christ in all persons and to respect the dignity of every human being"?[6] Although most of us would never consciously admit it, our behavior may nonetheless at times bear witness to this reality.

As one church was preparing for its annual Christmas bazaar, a harmless, disheveled, mentally ill parishioner walked back to the kitchen and offered to help with the food preparation. The woman was new in the community and eager to give to the church in a way that she could. A church worker for the bazaar told me in disbelief that a staff member had advised her to usher the woman out, because she was homeless and unbalanced. To be sure, some strangers may represent a possible danger to others and should be dealt with accordingly; however, this was not the case here. We do not expect this response to the stranger in a church that preaches love of neighbor and the inclusivity of God's love, yet it happens more often than any of us like to think.

What separates us as a Christian community is precisely how we welcome those who may be unwelcome in other settings. The Letter of James clearly states this central Christian belief. "For if a person with gold rings and in fine clothes comes into your assembly, and if a poor person in dirty clothes also comes in, and if you take notice of the one wearing the fine clothes and say, 'Have a seat here, please,' while to the one who is poor you say, 'Stand there,' or 'Sit at my feet,' have you not made distinctions among yourselves, and become judges with evil thoughts? Listen, my beloved brothers and sisters. Has not God chosen the poor in the world to be rich in faith and to be heirs of the kingdom that he has promised to those who love him?" (Jas 2:2–5).

It is abundantly clear throughout scripture that we are to extend hospitality to all strangers. How easy it is to welcome the young, nicely dressed family, with children in tow, who can offer their time to committee work and various church functions. But how about the many other strangers God sends our way? How about the elderly, the physically or the mentally disabled, the unwed couple living together, the couple recently married after a publicly known extramarital affair, the person with AIDS, the homosexual man or woman, the person recently released from prison, the white-collar criminal recently indicted on insider trading charges? How will we welcome these people? Will part of us, like the Mother Superior in *Sister Act*, turn away from our vows and say, "I lied"?

Our human predicaments are often mirrored in the world of nature. If we will look reflectively at this part of God's creation, we may find that unexpected gifts await us there. Our own struggle with the predicament of welcoming the unwelcomed is expressed in a poem by Mary Sammons Patton.

LINES TO STARLINGS ON A SNOWY DAY[7]

On a snowy day the starlings gather
Providing provocation to my soul!
And consternation grim!
They are ugly! They are stupid!
They are pushy! They are pigs!
Their greed is sickening.
Their name is Legion!
Their faults are multiplied.
They are revolting!
Their charms are nil! Totally uninhibited!
They make me ill!
"Shoo!" I say.
"You horrid bird!
Go away!"

But ah! the pretty redbird!
The cunning chickadee!
The winsome tiny titmice!
And all the lovely dainty
Fragile feathered friends!
I take joy and delight in preparing
sumptuous goodies
For these beauties!

I pause. With sudden revelation
I look at the starlings once more.
With all the bird-world, frozen,
And starving all are foraging, dependent.
Who am I to thus discriminate?
These unlovely, unloved creatures
Are God's own, too.
Who am I to so deny their desperate need?
And so I know I must and lovingly, feed—
Feed the starlings on a snowy day.

Mary Sammons Patton

Who are we to discriminate? Who are we to deny the desperate need of those who come our way? How are we not only to feed the strangers God sends our way, but to feed them lovingly, as the poem suggests?

Once again, we must look to our Judeo-Christian roots for guidance. For without a firm scriptural and theological understanding of why we as Christian people "feed the starlings lovingly," we run the risk of feeding them merely from a sense that we should help those less fortunate than we, or worse, from a sense of guilt.

Throughout the gospel narratives, Jesus "feeds the starlings lovingly" again and again. Jesus' hospitality to sinners and the unacceptable was a hallmark of his ministry. He regularly dined with tax collectors, the pariahs of his day, causing much trouble for himself, as well as for the word he was proclaiming (Mk 2:15–17; Lk 15:1–2). How could anyone who dined with tax collectors have a message that was worth receiving? Moreover, when the scribes and Pharisees brought the adulterous woman to Jesus, he did not condemn her but sided with her against those who found her unacceptable, again causing trouble for himself (Jn 8:2–11).

When Jesus read from the scroll of the prophet Isaiah, in the synagogue in Nazareth, he made it clear that his ministry was for everyone, especially the poor and oppressed. "The Spirit of the Lord is upon me, because he has anointed me to bring good news to the poor. He has sent me to proclaim release to the captives and recovery of sight to the blind, to let the oppressed go free, to proclaim the year of the Lord's favor" (Lk 4:18–19).

Jesus clearly felt he was sent to the poor and oppressed, among whom was the largest class of that group, women. The most oppressed of women were the widows, because they had no standing before the law, no one to provide for them, and almost no means of livelihood. Jesus demonstrates concern for and acceptance of widows in the story of the widow's mite (Lk 21:1–4; Mk 12:41–44); in his teaching regarding the scribes who "devour widows' houses" (Lk 20:45–47; Mk 12:38–40); in raising to life the only son of the widow of Nain (Lk 7:11–17); and in his teaching that Elijah was sent to a widow at Zarephath (Lk 4:25–27).[8]

Throughout his ministry, Jesus showed acceptance of many of society's outcasts. The woman who had been bleeding for twelve years was ritually unclean according to Jewish law (Lv 15:19–30), yet Jesus touched her and healed her (Mt 9:20–22; Mk 5:24–34; Lk 8:43–48). In healing the Gerasenes man possessed with demons and the ten people with leprosy, Jesus again touched those who were feared and ostracized by society (Lk 8:26–39; Lk 17:11–19). In his willingness to engage in conversation with the Samaritan woman at the well, Jesus broke several Jewish customs (Jn 4:5–30). Normally, not only would a Jew not address a Samaritan, but a man would not speak to a woman in public, especially if the man was a rabbi.[9]

As Jesus welcomed the outcast with open arms, so too have others followed in his footsteps. Where would Christianity be today if Ananias had not welcomed the outcast Paul into his faith community? Paul, who had openly persecuted Christians, was hardly an acceptable stranger of his day. In *New Testament Hospitality* John Koenig writes: "Paul's history as a believer begins with the residential disciple Ananias and the community at Damascus to which he belongs. Without this local church's courageous welcoming of its persecutor, there would have been no Christian Paul."[10] Furthermore, at the beginning of Paul's missionary career, his associates feared that he was a secret agent of the Jerusalem authorities. Even so, Barnabas, a member of the community, recommended him to the apostles (Acts 9:26–30). In the language of hospitality, Barnabas welcomed this volatile newcomer into the mainstream of the church's life.[11] It is difficult to think of Paul as a newcomer, yet he was—and an unacceptable one at that. He was volatile, on the fringe, and suspected of being a secret agent. Yet what gifts did this stranger bring, not only to those who welcomed him, but to all of Christendom.

Again, in the world of nature, Mary Sammons Patton sees this reality revealed.

TO A BULB[12]

Who would ever think
To look at you,
You brownish, ugly, shrivelled thing
That you hold within the depths
Of you
The very heart of Spring!

We often find the heart of spring, the gift of life, in the places we least expect to find it. In *Sister Act*, the very person the Mother Superior did not want to welcome ultimately became the answer to the prayers of an ailing inner-city congregation. Whoopi used her gifts of singing and teaching to give the convent choir a new voice, a new sound, a new spirit. As new life filled their lungs, new life was breathed into the dwindling congregation. Gradually, the pews began to fill, as the shriveled bulb burst forth into colorful song.

Those who offer hospitality to the stranger often receive far more than they give. How is it that those we welcome, even reluctantly, often welcome us in turn? As guests become hosts and hosts become guests, God's work within the sacred relationship of hospitality often becomes manifest.

Guest/Host Reversals

When we make the decision to welcome all strangers, we become a link in the chain of hospitality that reaches back through Sarah and Abraham, through Jesus and Ananias, through countless Christians throughout the centuries. When we make the decision to extend hospitality to another in the name of Christ, we enter into a sacred relationship where God is present. "For where two or three are gathered in my name, I am there among them" (Mt 18:20).

Jesus Christ, the Word made flesh, is the revelation of God in our midst. Jesus is the Word of God. The Word is God's ongoing self-communication, God's reaching out to humanity, God's revelation.[13] In *The Word of God and Pastoral Care*, Howard Stone writes: "God addresses us in the word; in the word we encounter the One who is indeed with us. This meeting of God and person in the word has about it a sense of call—the call into relationship."[14]

When we are called into relationship with the stranger, we are called to be hosts in the truest sense of the word. Margaret Guenther's *Holy Listening* notes that the German words for "host" perhaps convey this depth of meaning better than the English. *Gastgeber* means "the guest-giver," the one who gives to guests, and *Gastfreundschaft* denotes a guest-friendship, the special friendship that is shown by hosts to guests. As we welcome the stranger, we are called to be bestowers of such guest-friendship, reflecting the warm hospitality shown by the host at the heavenly banquet.[15] As we are called into relationship with another, we are called to extend this special friendship. As we reach out in the name of Christ in this act of friendship, we can become both bearers and receivers of the word of God.

It is the awareness of the presence of God within such relationships that enables us to be not only hosts, but guests. For this to occur when we enter into dialogue with the stranger, we need to participate in mutual listening. We must be willing not only to give in the name of Christ, but to receive in the name of Christ as well, for what often comes to us in and through the other's utterances is nothing less than God's word for us.[16]

This guest/host reversal is vividly depicted in the story of Abraham's welcoming of the three heavenly strangers in Genesis 18:1–15. Abraham literally runs from his tent to meet them, bows down, and then offers them water, rest, and food. As they are eating the meal prepared for them, one of the strangers reveals God's word to Sarah and Abraham. Sarah is to have a son in her old age.

In reflecting on this passage from Genesis, the author of Hebrews wrote: "Let mutual love continue. Do not neglect to show hospitality to strangers, for by doing that some have entertained angels without knowing it" (Heb 13:1–2). Just as these angels were God's messengers to Sarah and Abraham, the angels God sends to us today are God's messengers.

A similar guest/host reversal is found in Luke's Gospel following the passion narrative, when two people on the road to Emmaus encounter a stranger. They act as host to him, telling their story of the death of the Messiah; then they listen as the stranger shares his knowledge of scripture regarding the role of the messiah (Lk 24:13–27). As they come to the village to which they are going, the stranger walks ahead as if he is going on. "But they urged him strongly, saying, 'Stay with us, because it is almost evening and the day is now nearly over' " (Lk 24:29). It is through this act of welcoming the stranger into their home for the breaking of bread that they learn it is Jesus to whom they are speaking. The hosts to the stranger become the guests of Christ. As guests, they are able to hear God's word for them. If they had never reached out to this stranger, how different their lives would have been.

The host, as receiver of God's gifts from the stranger is lyrically portrayed in an old Gaelic rune:

> I saw a stranger yestreen;
> I put food in the eating place,
> Drink in the drinking place,
> Music in the listening place;
> And in the blessed name of the Triune
> he blessed myself and my house,
> my cattle and my dear ones.
> And the lark said in her song
>   Often, often, often,
> Goes the Christ in the stranger's guise;
>   Often, often, often,
> Goes the Christ in the stranger's guise.

Welcoming the Christ in the stranger's guise is deeply rooted in our biblical tradition. In addition to the encounter with Christ as the stranger on the road to Emmaus, is the narration of Christ's appearance as a gardener to Mary Magdalene as she stands weeping outside his tomb (Jn 20:11–18). Had she not spoken with this stranger, she would have never known that, in fact, it was the risen Christ to whom she was speaking. In Matthew 25, Jesus tells us that such instances are not restricted to his resurrection appearances, but occur in everyday life. In the parable of the sheep and the goats, the righteous ask him, "When was it that we saw you a stranger and welcomed you?" And he answered them, "Truly I tell you, just as you did it to one of the least of these who are members of my family, you did it to me" (Mt 25:31–46). Hospitality to the stranger was a hallmark of the kingdom of God in Jesus' day, just as it is today—"often, often, often goes the Christ in the stranger's guise."

Many times in my own life I have offered hospitality to the stranger and have been surprised by God's word for me, revealed through that person. Regardless of how often this happens, I am always filled with wonder when it does. Such guest/host reversals occurred frequently when I was working at Martin House, an inner-city Catholic settlement house in Trenton, New Jersey. I believed I was called there to teach, but I soon learned that I was there not so much to teach as to learn, not so much to change as to be changed. The teaching was more of a dialogue in which both parties had much to give and to be given.

I remember vividly one morning when one of my students was particularly agitated. She was a middle-aged woman who had been homeless most of her adult life. I took Emma into another room to talk, where used clothing was stored for resale in the community. She stood in the midst of the musty boxes piled high, in clothes she had worn for two weeks. Her eyes were often glazed and seemed to be searching in a far-off place, but they were very alert and alive at that moment. She told me over and over that someday people would not judge her by her outward appearance, but would see her for the type of person she was and for the type of heart she had. She just stood there, patting her heart, repeating these words to me. At that moment, my eye was drawn to a small glass ball that hung from a chain around her neck. It was about the size of a dime and contained one tiny seed. "Emma, what is this?" I asked. "That's a mustard seed," she replied. "That's what keeps me going, and keeps me knowing, that someday things will be different."

Emma lived out the message of Jesus to his disciples in Matthew 17, putting it at the center of her life. When the disciples were unable to heal a boy with epilepsy, they asked Jesus privately, "Why could we not cast it out?" He said to them, "Because of your little faith. For truly I tell you, if you have faith the size of a mustard seed, you will say to this mountain, 'Move from here to there,' and it will move; and nothing will be impossible for you" (Mt 17:19–21).

I learned as much about faith from that one conversation with Emma as I could have learned from reading books or listening to sermons. God's word for me was clear, as I learned what it meant to receive the word of God from someone I thought was there to learn from me. When we receive another in the name of Christ and believe in mutual listening for the word of God, we will be surprised again and again by the many angels God sends our way. For as Henri Nouwen writes in *Reaching Out: The Three Movements of the Spiritual Life*, "Reaching out to strangers is not just reaching out to the long row of people who are so obviously needy—in need of food, clothing and of many forms of care—but also a reaching out to the promises they are bringing with them as gifts to their host."[17]

To be open to receive these gifts, we must be willing to leave our own safe place and to let ourselves be guided. Abba James of the desert knew it was easier to be the host than the guest, when he wrote, "It is better to receive hospitality than to offer it."[18] Those who find it easier to reach out to others than to let some-

one reach out to them would do well to heed his words, for without the willingness to let God work within our encounters with
strangers, we will miss the gifts they bring to us.

This guest/host reversal and the gifts imparted within the sacred relationship based on hospitality is contained within the
Greek word for "hospitality" *philoxenia*, used in the New
Testament. This word refers not only to a love and acceptance of
strangers, but to a delight in the whole guest/host relationship,
in the mysterious reversals and gains for both parties that may
occur. For those who believe, this delight is fueled by the expectation that God will play a role in the guest/host encounter.[19] It
is such mysterious reversals that both delight and instruct those
who are open to receive God's word from the Christ in the
stranger's guise.

Chapter 2

HOSPITALITY THROUGH STORY-LISTENING

As we focus on the many ways of offering hospitality to the stranger, it is helpful to begin from the vantage point of our own experience as a stranger. God suggests such remembering to the Israelites during the exodus. "You shall not oppress a stranger; you know the heart of a stranger, for you were strangers in the land of Egypt" (Ex 23:9 RSV). When we were the stranger, what was in our heart? Who welcomed us and what did they do? How did we feel when they reached out to us, enveloping us in the warmth of hospitality?

Chances are, whoever reached us, found us where we were at that particular time in our lives. For the people who not only reach out to us, but find us, are those who meet us where we are—not where they are, or where they wish we were, but exactly where we happen to be at that moment. Because every human being has a fundamental need to be understood, the people whose hospitality we feel most comfortable accepting are usually those we feel can understand us.

How can we communicate that level of understanding to the many strangers God sends our way? First of all, we can listen to them. In Taylor Caldwell's book *The Listener*, she writes, "The most desperate need of people today is not . . . a new religion, or a new 'way of life.' . . . People's real need, their most terrible need, is for someone to listen to them, not as a 'patient,' but as a human soul. They need to tell someone of what they think, of the bewilderment they encounter when they try to discover why they were born, how they must live and where their destiny lies."[1] In caring enough to listen to another's story, we communicate an interest in that person as an individual. Only through listening to others can we learn who they are and where they are

33

on their journey, enabling us to meet them exactly where they are.

In Geoffrey Chaucer's *The Canterbury Tales*, the Host, one of the characters in the book, offers us a constructive model for extending hospitality to strangers through story-listening. In this poem, written in the Middle Ages, twenty-nine people are accidentally brought together at the Tabard, a hostelry in Southwark, England. They are all pilgrims on their way to Canterbury to visit the site of the martyrdom of St. Thomas á Becket. They are strangers to one another, as well as to their Host at the Tabard. Although all the pilgrims could have proceeded to Canterbury in their own individual groups, the Host brings them together for mutual support and enjoyment along their journey.

Chaucer writes: "Our Host welcomed each of us with open arms and soon led us to our places at the supper-table. . . . 'Ladies and gentlemen,' began the Host, 'do yourselves a good turn and listen to what I say, and please don't turn up your noses at it. This is the point in a nutshell: each of you, to make the road seem shorter, shall tell two stories on the journey. . . . And just to make it the more fun for you I'll gladly ride with you myself at my own cost and be your guide. . . . Now if you agree, let me know here and now without more ado, and I'll make my arrangements early.' . . . Next morning our Host rose up at break of day, roused us all and gathered us together in a flock."[2]

In offering hospitality to strangers, the Host in *The Canterbury Tales*, did not merely say, "Welcome, I'm glad you're here," and then leave them on their own. First, he welcomed each of them with open arms and offered them a meal, during which he suggested that they all tell stories along their journey. Next, he let them decide whether they wanted to do this, giving them a choice. Then, quite importantly, he offered to go with them himself to be their guide.

We who are hosts are all guides to the pilgrims God sends our way. We are not meant to welcome the stranger in the name of Christ and then leave. In Gloria Purka's *Praying with Julian of Norwich*, she writes: "The nature of a pilgrimage is such that transformation occurs not at the end of the trip but in the making of the journey."[3] Our call as Christians is to be companions along this journey. And how are we to do this? Much as the Host in *The Canterbury Tales* did, by urging others to share a story with us and by listening to what they say. As the Host listened to the "once upon a time" stories, he learned much about the storytellers and where they were as pilgrims on their own faith journeys, even though their stories were not about themselves. So, too, can we learn by listening to the strangers God sends our way, by inviting them to share a story with us.

It is interesting that although the Host listens to all of the pilgrim's stories, actively engaging them in response, he never tells his own story. Thus, the Host is both a welcomer and a story-listener, rather than a storyteller.

Becoming a good story-listener is at the heart of being a good host. In Henri Nouwen's *Reaching Out: The Three Movements of the Spiritual Life* he writes: "Someone who is filled with ideas, concepts, opinions and convictions cannot be a good host. There is no inner space to listen, no openness to discover the gift of the other. . . . A good host not only has to be poor in mind but also poor in heart. When our heart is filled with prejudices, worries, jealousies, there is little room for a stranger."[4] Being able to receive others and provide a hospitable space for them requires self-emptying on the part of the host. Without such self-emptying, there is no room to let another in.[5]

Nowhere in scripture is this point more profoundly made than in the Book of Job. Following the deaths of all of Job's children and the loss of all he had, his three friends try to console him. Rather than merely listening to his story, they each offer him their wisdom and advice. Job finally says, "What you know, I also know; I am not inferior to you. . . . If you would only keep silent, that would be your wisdom!" (Jb 13:2, 5). Keeping silent is indeed a wisdom, a virtue that all hosts should cultivate if they are to offer hospitable space to the angels God sends their way.

A parishioner named Leigh recently told me of an experience she had with a good story-listener who was able to offer hospitality to her in this time-honored way. She was in one of the side chapels of her church, praying silently before a communion service that she expected to begin soon. Several rows behind her, she noticed a parishioner named Chris, whom she recognized but did not know, who was also praying. As time passed and no one else entered the church, Leigh decided she had the time of the service wrong. Knowing that she had some free time, she allowed herself to experience the painful feelings she was praying about; then her tears began to flow as these emotions came over her. She suddenly felt a hand on her shoulder, as the parishioner behind her asked, "Would you like some company, or would you like to be alone?" This host-parishioner gave her a choice. Leigh then offered Chris a seat next to her. After some time spent in silent communion, Leigh said, "I've prayed for months for healing, yet nothing has happened." "Are you sick?" Chris asked. "No, no. I'm praying for healing because my twin brother was suddenly killed in a car accident last year. Yesterday was the first anniversary of his death." As the story poured forth, Leigh noticed tears running down Chris's face—tears of compassion and concern for her woundedness. Through story-listening, Chris, as host, was able to meet her exactly where she was at that moment on her journey. Leigh later described the experience to me as a grace-filled gift from God.

As we offer hospitality to others, one of our first tasks is indeed to listen. Listening to the life experience of another, with the purpose of understanding it as deeply as possible, enables the listener to discern what God has already been doing in that person's life. In *Proclamation as Offering:Story and Choice*, Wayne Schwab and William Yon state: "In practice, listening rather than telling is the usual beginning point in evangelization."[6] It is through story-listening that we will be able to meet the strangers where they are, and it is through story-listening that we have the greatest chance of being received by them as well.

Being received by the stranger through story-listening is poignantly portrayed in *The Yellow Wind* by David Grossman. This book brings the reader into the thoughts and feelings of Palestinians in the refugee camps in Israel today. Grossman, an Israeli Jew, reaches out in hospitality to his Arab neighbors, who in turn receive him just as hospitably.

One day he visits a group of refugees who miraculously have been able to return from a refugee camp to their native village, which they were forced to evacuate twenty-four years earlier. Grossman writes, "We are sheltered in a shady, broad yard, and the little valley lies at our feet, and the storage pools sparkle in the sun, and despite the Ramadan fast, my hosts bring me a glass of tea, and little by little people from every corner of the village gather around us, listening, nodding their heads, and telling their stories—but not freely."[7]

Not only do the Palestinians welcome Grossman into their homes, they break one of their own holy day fasts to offer him a glass of tea. As the guest is welcomed by the Arab hosts, he moves into the role of host himself, through careful story-listening. Traditionally insurmountable barriers come tumbling down through this time-honored way of extending hospitality to another.

Henry Ralph Carse, a Christian living in Israel, relates a similar incident in which he is welcomed hospitably by strangers on a Christmas eve in Bethlehem, just after the six day war.

On Christmas Eve, I walked to Bethlehem, naively expecting to attend the Midnight Mass. From Jerusalem to the very threshold of the Basilica of the Nativity, the roads were crowded with the limousines of ecclesiastical and otherwise distinguished personalities. At the church, all the entrances were heavily guarded by Israeli security forces; only visitors armed with special passes could gain entrance.

It was nearly midnight. Once I had left the crush of activity in Manger Square I found the narrow streets of Bethlehem very quiet. I wandered aimlessly, beginning to feel thoroughly chilled, wondering in my innocence if I would find a youth hostel. Instead, I passed a narrow lighted doorway, and turned to enter it, hearing a cheerful levantine "Welcome!" from within. It was a tiny barber shop of sorts, and there indeed was the elderly proprietor giving a young man what I suppose was a well-lathered Turkish shave. Immediately I was made to feel at ease, offered a low stool and showered with curious questions. The shave was abandoned, three cups of very hot sweet tea were produced from the shadows, and our rough conversation turned, naturally enough, to religion.

My hosts were, they informed me, Moslems, but not, of course, they assured me hurriedly, the kind who don't shave. Not feeling particularly enlightened by this disclosure, I asked them how they felt about the big birthday celebrations which had turned their home town into an international V.I.P. event. They laughed, and the younger man said, "This is nothing. You heard how Prophet Mohammed born?" Of course I hadn't.

In the stillest, smallest hours of Christmas Day, in a Bethlehem barber shop, I listened in fascination to the miraculous birth tale of Allah's messenger. The two men

shared in the telling, vying to improve each other's English
delivery, drawn by my listening into a strange excitement,
reaching for half-remembered details which would give the
story oriental perfection. Their voices, their faces, reflected
not only pride and confidence, but something like relief; it
was exactly as if they had been waiting a long time for
someone who had never heard. . . .[8]

As the Moslems welcomed this young man and shared hot tea
with him, little did they know of the gifts this stranger was
bringing for them. Here, as in the story by David Grossman,
story-listening bridges cultural, language, and faith differences.
Similarly, listening can bridge differences for us also, if we let
others know that we care enough to listen to them. For how
many people, like the men in this story, are just waiting for
someone who has never heard?

As we become hosts to the many pilgrims God sends our way,
in hope of being received by them, a conscious effort to develop
our skills as story-listeners may be needed. For some, this gift
comes almost naturally. For others, specific training is helpful, as
fortunately the art of story-listening can be both taught and
practiced. For this purpose, there is a Listening Skills Workshop
at the end of this chapter that I have used over the last eight
years to introduce various lay groups to this aspect of hospitality
ministry. It can serve as an introduction to the art of listening.[9]
Because as Christians we should be engaged not only in story-listening, but also in mutual listening for the word of God, the
focus in the workshop is on both.

Listening Skills Workshop

Session 1
Story-Listening

Materials Needed:	Newsprint and marker
	Paper and pen for each participant
Handouts:	2A—"Roadblocks to Effective Communication" p. 42.
	2B—"Positive Story-Listening Skills" p. 43.
Quotation:	"What you know, I also know; I am not inferior to you. . . . If you would only keep silent, that would be your wisdom!" (Jb 13:2, 5)

1. Before the session, write the quotation on newsprint and save it for later. Begin with a warm-up exercise. Give everyone a piece of paper and a pen. Tell participants to write what their response would be to a person with the following problem. Tell them no one will see their answers. The exercise is just for them to learn more about how they respond to people in need.[10]

a. A thirteen-year-old girl comes home from school and says, "Nobody likes me. I've got braces and I had to walk home from school by myself. I wasn't invited to Mary's party and I feel terrible. Nobody likes me."

b. Your spouse, or a good friend, says to you, "I just don't think I can take it at work one more day. Two people were fired last month. Now I'm supposed to do my job plus theirs! I feel as though my boss is really taking advantage of me. I had to work fifty-five hours last week just to get everything done. I can't keep this up. I'm exhausted."[11]

c. A widowed friend calls you and says, "Ever since Bill died, life seems to have lost all meaning for me. I'm so lonely and depressed I just don't see the point of living any more."

2. Next discuss the role of host as story-listener, as described on page 35. State that people who are serious about offering hospitality to another may want to work at developing good listening skills. Read aloud the following quotation by Taylor Caldwell: "The most desperate need of people today is not . . . a new reli-

gion, or a new 'way of life.' . . . People's real need, their most terrible need, is for someone to listen to them, not as a 'patient,' but as a human soul. They need to tell someone of what they think, of the bewilderment they encounter when they try to discover why they were born, how they must live and where their destiny lies."[11] Tell participants that they already know a great deal about listening and being listened to because they have been involved in one or the other most of their lives.

3. Have the group brainstorm answers to the question: "What happens in a conversation when you feel the other person is not listening to you? What do they do or not do?" For example, if a person is looking somewhere else when you are talking to them, you may feel they are not listening. Write participants' answers on newsprint.

4. Give out the "Roadblocks to Effective Communication" handout on page 42. You might want to have the headings written on newsprint. Discuss, pointing out where the group's answers to the previous question overlap the answers given on the handout. Tell them that nearly everyone will include some roadblocks in their answers to the first exercise. Have them look back at these answers. Then make the point that this list of roadblocks applies only to situations in which one person is upset and needs to express her or his feelings. This does not apply to every situation involving communication. Use your own examples to highlight each point.

Roadblock 3 is one of the most common. If we tell someone else what to do, it suggests that we know more than she or he does. Show the quotation from Job written on newsprint at this time. Suggest participants write it down and keep it. State that one of the most important things they can learn from this workshop is that *they cannot solve someone else's problems*. They should let people talk out their problems themselves, as they listen, and eventually each person will come up with their own solution. Realizing and believing that God did not put us here to solve other people's problems can be a very freeing experience.

Coffee Break for 10 minutes

5. Now that you have discussed what *not* to do in listening, it is important to discuss what *to* do. Distribute copies of the handout "Positive Skills for Story-Listening." You might want to have the headings written on newsprint. Discuss these skills, giving examples as you go.

6. Divide participants into groups of three. Each group will have a story-teller, a story-listener, and an observer. The role of the observer is to make notes of the roadblocks to communications and the positive listening skills used. The story-teller can use one of the examples from the warm-up exercise, acting out the role of the person with the problem. After five minutes, have the observers report what they have noticed. Switch roles. Each person should have a chance to be storyteller, story-listener, and observer.

7. Ask everyone to come back together in the large group. Invite people to share their experiences. You may want to close with the following quotation from *Reaching Out* by Henri Nouwen. This ministry "points to someone higher than our thoughts can reach, someone deeper than our hearts can feel and wider than our arms can embrace, someone under whose wings we can find refuge (Psalm 90) and in whose love we can rest, someone we call our God."[12]

Tell the group that in the next session the focus will be on the role of God in our ministry as story-listeners.

ROADBLOCKS TO EFFECTIVE COMMUNICATION

1. *Warning, promising*
   Telling the person what consequences will occur if he does something.

2. *Moralizing, preaching*
   Telling the person what she should or ought to do.

3. *Advising, giving solutions or suggestions*
   Telling the person how to solve a problem, giving advice, providing answers or solutions.

4. *Judging, criticizing, disagreeing, blaming*
   Making a negative judgment or evaluation of the person.

5. *Praising*
   Offering a positive evaluation.

6. *Ridiculing, shaming*
   Making the person feel foolish, putting him in a category.

7. *Interpreting, analyzing, diagnosing*
   Telling the person what her or someone else's motives are, playing "shrink."

8. *Reassuring, sympathizing, supporting*
   Trying to make the person feel better, talking him out of his feelings, trying to make those feelings go away, denying the strength of his feelings.

9. *Probing, questioning, interrogating*
   Trying to find reasons, motives, causes; searching for more information to help *you* solve the problem.

10. *Withdrawing, distracting, diverting*
    Trying to get the person away from the problem, withdrawing from the problem yourself, pushing the problem aside.

Adapted from Thomas Gordon, *Parent Effectiveness Training*, New York: Peter H. Wyden, Inc., 1970, 42-44. Used by permission.

HANDOUT 2A

POSITIVE SKILLS FOR STORY-LISTENING

1. *Silence accompanied by appropriate nonverbal behavior*
Leaning forward

   Maintaining eye contact

   Nodding head

   Nonjudgmental facial expression

2. *Noncommittal acknowledgments*
"Mm hmmm."

   "Oh."

   "I see."

   "Interesting."

3. *Door openers*
"Tell me about it."

   "Would you like to talk about it?"

   "Sounds as though you've got some deep feelings about that."

   "Tell me more."

   "I'd like to hear about it."

4. *Paraphrasing—Lets the person know you understand him or her*
"You feel . . ."

   "It seems to you that . . ."

   "You think . . ."

   "What I hear you saying is . . ."

   "I'm picking up that you . . ."

5. *Perception checking—Useful when you are having some difficulty perceiving correctly. Helps the person feel cared for and understood.*
"Correct me if I'm wrong, but . . ."

   "This is what I think I hear you saying . . ."

   "You appear to be feeling . . ."

HANDOUT 2B

"I'm not sure whether I'm with you; do you mean? . . ."

"I'm not certain I understand; you're saying . . ."

6. *Reflecting gut-level feelings*
"Sounds as though you're very angry about that."

"You feel hurt."

"It sounds as if you're frustrated."

Acknowledgments and door openers adapted from Thomas Gordon, *Parent Effectiveness Training*, New York: Peter H. Wyden, Inc., 1970, 47–48. Used by permission.

Session 2
Mutual Listening For God's Word

Materials Needed:	Newsprint and marker
Handouts:	2C—"Angels," page 47.
	2D—"Rune of Hospitality," page 49.
	2E—*Christ Appearing as a Gardener to Mary Magdalene*, page 50.
Quotation:	"For where two or three are gathered in my name, I am there among them" (Mt 18:20).

It is best if each participant can have her or his own copy of *The Word of God and Pastoral Care* by Howard Stone (Abingdon Press, 1988), to reinforce the teachings of this workshop.

1. Begin by having the group sing "Angels" together. If possible arrange for guitar accompaniment or play the song on a cassette, which can be ordered (see page 48 for details).

2. Ask one participant to read aloud Genesis 18:1–15. Then have another read Luke 24:13–27. Discuss the guest/host reversals found in these stories in light of pages 28-32 in Chapter 1.

3. Read aloud the "Rune of Hospitality," then give a copy of it to each person. Next, distribute copies of the Rembrandt drawing, *Christ Appearing as a Gardener to Mary Magdalene*. Discuss the concept of Christ in the stranger's guise. State that reaching out to strangers is not just reaching out to people who may need our help. It is "also a reaching out to the promises they are bringing with them as gifts to their host."[13]

4. Write the Greek word for "hospitality," *philoxenia*, on newsprint. State that this word refers not only to a love and acceptance of strangers, but also to a delight in the whole guest/host relationship, in the mysterious reversals and gains for both parties that may occur. For those who believe, this delight is fueled by the expectation that God will play a role in the guest/host encounter.[14]

Tell participants that for them to be both bearers and receivers of the word of God in their encounter with the other, they must participate in *mutual listening*. They must be willing not only to give in the name of Christ, but to receive in the name of Christ as well, for what will often come to them in and through the other's utterances is nothing less than God's word for them.[15] In mutual listening, they need to realize that *they are God's gift to the other person, and that person is also God's gift to them.* This realization is what moves their story-listening from the realm of the secular to the sacred. It is mutual listening for the word of God, revealed through another, that makes their encounter a pastoral one.

5. Repeat Exercise 6 in Session 1. This time, ask each of the participants to focus on the concept of God in their midst. Read aloud the quotation given at the beginning of the workshop. Have group members focus on mutual listening, as well as their story-listening skills. Let storytellers choose one of the "problems" from the "Newcomer Scenario" handout on page 91. Do the exercise as before, except this time allow each person ten minutes to be the storyteller.

6. Gather as a group to reflect on the following question: "What was the difference between our role-play exercise today and the role play in our last session?"

Note: I recommend three or four more sessions, one month apart, using Exercise 4. Participants can make up and bring their own sample problems. It is best if participants do not use real issues from their own lives in the role plays.

ANGELS

Words and music by Patrick Powers

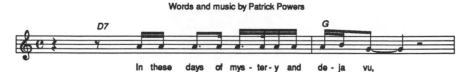

In these days of mys - ter - y and de - ja vu,

nev - er know - ing who we might just bump in - to, co -

in - cid - ence, in - cid - ents when who knows who might be talk- ing to an

an-gel. Nev - er know - ing whom we might be list- 'ning to,

an - gels could be drop - ping in on me and you.

May - be you're the an - gel; we need ears for you, you saints and

an - gels. And the an - gels sang, "Glo -

* Patrick Powers
From the play *ANGELS*

Reprinted with the permission of Patrick Powers from his play, *ANGELS*, about angels in a business environment. Cassette tapes of this song can be ordered by sending $6.00 to:

   Patrick Powers
   75 Line Road
   Hamilton Township, NJ 08690

HANDOUT 2C (continued)

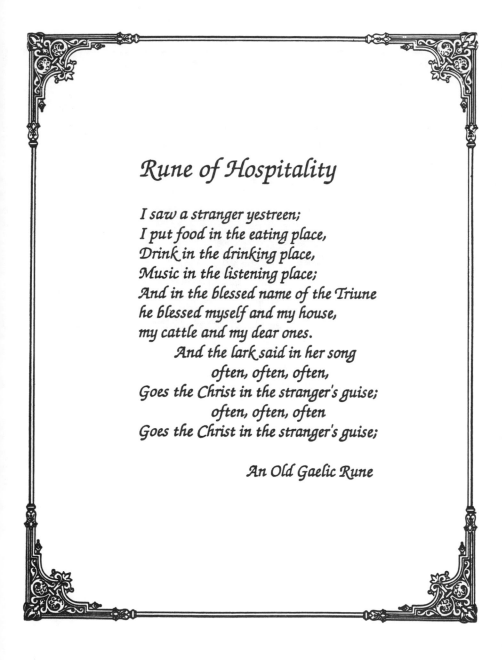

Rune of Hospitality

I saw a stranger yestreen;
I put food in the eating place,
Drink in the drinking place,
Music in the listening place;
And in the blessed name of the Triune
he blessed myself and my house,
my cattle and my dear ones.
And the lark said in her song
often, often, often,
Goes the Christ in the stranger's guise;
often, often, often
Goes the Christ in the stranger's guise;

An Old Gaelic Rune

CHRIST APPEARING AS A GARDENER TO MARY MAGDALENE.
Rembrandt. Circa 1643. Amsterdam.

PART II

Chapter 3

CREATING AN EFFECTIVE NEWCOMER PROGRAM

At a newcomer workshop I was giving last year, I began with my usual question, "What led you to this particular church?" One couple related that they had stumbled upon the church quite by accident. "Shortly after we moved here, we saw a sign for another church in this denomination, St. Mary's in the Field. We asked about it and heard it was a friendly, caring place, so we decided to give it a try. On the way to St. Mary's, our car suddenly ran out of gas directly in front of *this* church! The ten o'clock service was about to begin, so we just locked the car and went in. I don't know whether it was an act of God or what, but we've been coming here ever since and we couldn't be happier."

To be sure, people may first enter the doors of our church for a variety of reasons—some quite unanticipated. Regardless of how newcomers find their way to us, once they arrive it is our call to extend hospitality to them in the name of Christ. This involves more than just offering an initial welcome. As we welcome others into the body of Christ, it is important that we engage in story-listening. In addition, intentional follow-up through a newcomer program is essential in today's church.

Research has shown that effective newcomer programs vary, depending on the size of the congregation. In *Sizing Up a Congregation*, Arlin Rothauge divides churches into four groups: the family church with 50 active members, the pastoral church of 50 to 150 members, the program church of 150 to 350 members, and the corporation church of 350 to 500 or more members.[1] Successful hospitality ministries in program and corporation churches are similar and will be addressed first. Alterations to this more comprehensive type of undertaking will then be discussed in light of the needs of family- and pastoral-size churches.

Successful newcomer programs differ from church to church, but at their heart lie two key elements: a willingness of church members to offer hospitality through story-listening, and lay ownership and involvement in the program. Laity need a theological background for hospitality ministry, consciousness raising about newcomer needs, and a chance to develop their own program. For this reason, a workshop is offered in Chapter 5 to enable this involvement to develop. Moreover, effective newcomer programs contain a number of other key components: greeting, tracking, calling, orienting, and integrating newcomers handled in a systematic, yet caring way.

The Role of Hospitality Ministers

To begin, program and corporation churches may want to have greeters at each entrance on Sunday mornings. Because the word *greeter* can imply a kind of glad-hand approach, I prefer to use the term *hospitality minister*, for such a person is far more than a mere welcomer in the secular sense. Hospitality ministers may be commissioned at a worship service, for such an offering of one's time is indeed a lay ministry.[2] It is best to schedule these lay ministers for four weeks in a row. By the second or third Sunday, they will be familiar with who is new and who is not. In addition, they will be able to recognize newcomers who may be attending on their second or third visits.

In liturgical churches it is helpful for hospitality ministers to ask whether a visitor is familiar with the liturgy. If not, it is best to seat the person next to a parishioner who can help the visitor find his or her way through the service. In *Church Growth and the Power of Evangelism*, Howard Hanchey relates a humorous story, written by Michael Deaver, that highlights the difficulties encountered by visitors who are not familiar with the service of Holy Communion in an Episcopal Church. In this story, the visitors happen to be Nancy and Ronald Reagan.

The Episcopal service is somewhat more formal, with kneeling and a common chalice and considerably more ritual. This kind of Mass was very foreign to the Reagans and within minutes after we were inside the church they kept sending nervous glances my way. They were turning pages of the prayer book as fast as they could, and I was handing them loose pages to help them keep up.

Nancy whispered to me in a mildly frantic voice, "Mike, what are we supposed to do?" I explained the ceremony as quickly and as confidently as I could: how we would walk to the altar and kneel, the minister would pass by with the wine (the blood of Christ), and the wafers (the body of Christ). He would bless them and keep moving.

The president, who as most people know has a slight hearing problem, leaned toward us but picked up little of what I was saying.

We started toward the altar and halfway down the aisle I felt Nancy Reagan clutch my arm. In front of us, all I could see were people crossing themselves and genuflecting. "Mike!" She hissed. "Are those people drinking out of the same cup?"

You have to remember that Nancy is the daughter of a doctor. I said, "It's all right. They'll come by with the wafers first. Then, when the chalice reaches you, dip the bread in the cup and that is perfectly all right. You won't have to put your lips to the cup."

The president said, "What? What?"

Nancy said, "Ron, just do exactly as I do."

Unknown to me, the church had made its wafers out of unleavened bread, which gave them the look and hardness of Jewish matzoh. Nancy selected a square of bread, and when the chalice came by she dipped hers . . . and dropped it. The square sank in the wine. She looked at me with huge eyes.

By then the trays had reached the president. Very calmly, and precisely, he picked up a piece of unleavened bread and dropped it in the wine. I watched the minister move on, shaking his head, staring at these blobs of gunk in his wine.

Nancy was relieved to leave the church. The president was chipper as he stepped into the sunlight, satisfied that the service had gone quite well.[3]

Those of us who are long-time members of liturgical churches need to be reminded of how bewildering such worship can be for those who are attending for the first time. Just as Nancy Reagan was "relieved to leave the church," how many visitors are relieved to leave our churches after fumbling through leaflets,

prayer books, and hymnals? Imagine, too, their confusion concerning the numerous traditions that are distinct within such
denominations. It is helpful for such churches to raise the consciousness of parishioners, encouraging them to willingly volunteer their assistance if the person next to them seems to be
confused.

After the service, hospitality ministers can return to the
doors, inviting all newcomers to attend coffee hour or adult education events. During such events, it is important for all
parishioners to wear name tags. A board with grooves can be
used to alphabetize pin-on name tags with plastic jackets.
Another method is to use name tags in plastic jackets with a
string attached, to be worn around the neck. These tags can be
hung on hooks, with all the As on one hook, all the Bs on another, and so on. Whichever method is used, it is best if newcomer tags are of a different color from those of church
members so that they can be easily located. In addition, it is
helpful for the name tag table or board to be staffed by two
parishioners, enabling them to greet new people warmly, as well
as to introduce them to members of the church. Information
about upcoming parish events can also be kept near the name
tags and given to all visitors.

At St. Columba's in Washington, D.C., rather than printing
the familiar reminder in their Sunday bulletin about coffee hour
following the service, they write: "There is hospitality after every
service—coffee in the Great Hall after all services and iced tea
in the Common after 10:15."[4] What a different focus is provided
by the statement that it is hospitality that is really being offered,
not merely coffee or tea. Such a notice also serves as a valuable
reminder to established church members.

Unfortunately, it can happen during coffee hour that new
people are left standing alone while church members talk to one
another. The pastor of a church in California illustrates a solution to this problem. "We organized 'secret hosts.' As the crowd
moves from the sanctuary into the coffee hour after worship,
these three or four couples watch for people who are standing
alone, talking to nobody."[5] After spotting people who are standing alone, these secret hosts accompany them into coffee hour,
visit with the newcomers, and then introduce them to other
parishioners. This helps break the cycle of unintentional exclu-
sivity that can develop in parishes.

Act of Friendship Tablet and Lay Calling

In any hospitality program it is critical to obtain the name and address of every visitor, every Sunday morning. In a large church, even the pew card method, hospitality ministers at the doors, and well-staffed name tag areas cannot secure the names of all visitors. To do so, the most fail-proof, least intrusive method I have found is the use of an Act of Friendship tablet, passed during the announcements in the worship service. See page 67 for a sample copy.

A friendship tablet serves two different functions in program and corporation churches. First, it supplies the church with an immediate list of all newcomers in attendance that morning. Second, it gives people in each pew a chance to know who the newcomers are and to welcome them accordingly. The concept of a friendship tablet may seem too "folksy" to some congregations when it is first mentioned. However, even well-established liturgical churches have found that the merits far outweigh the brief time it takes to become accustomed to its use.

At the end of the Sunday morning service, the Act of Friendship tablet can be used to compile a list of all first-time visitors. It is best for each one to receive a call from a lay visitor that same afternoon. Herb Miller in *How to Build a Magnetic Church* gives these statistics: "When lay persons make fifteen-minute visits to the homes of first-time worship visitors within thirty-six hours, 85 percent of them return the following week. Make this home visit within seventy-two hours, and 60 percent of them return. Make it seven days later, and 15 percent will return."[6] *By waiting merely one week to make our initial visit, we risk losing 70 percent of the strangers God sends our way.* Interestingly, this research also found that if clergy make this call, rather than laypersons, the results are each cut in half.[7] Thus, an effective lay calling system is indeed the cornerstone of an effective newcomer program.

It is important to keep in mind that growth is not the objective. Rather, offering hospitality to all who come our way is the goal. When hospitality is not immediately extended beyond an in-church welcome, the strangers God sends our way may be lost. These lost strangers are God's children, God's lost gift to us. These lost strangers are our responsibility. To meet this responsibility requires an effective, responsive calling system.

At Trinity Cathedral in San Francisco, hospitality ministers follow specific guidelines for calling. "If invited in, they never stay longer than fifteen minutes. *'Be bright, be brief, be gone' is the rule.*"[8] This motto, typed at the top of each caller's list, is all the training that is needed beyond the Hospitality Ministry Workshop in Chapter 5. For these brief visits it is best not to telephone in advance, because the answer is nearly always, "I'm fine. A visit isn't necessary."

Hospitality ministers for a given Sunday can serve as both greeters and callers. Grace Episcopal Church in Paducah, Kentucky, uses this method. On Sunday afternoon, the Sunday morning hospitality ministers take a nicely wrapped loaf of bread to the newcomer's home. If the person is not there, they simply leave the bread with a short note attached that includes the caller's name and telephone number. Bradley Tate, a hospitality minister in this program, stated in an interview: "It is much easier to knock on a stranger's door if you have something like bread to give them. It gives you a purpose for being there, other than merely saying, 'We're glad you came!' It is also symbolic of offering them the body of Christ, which adds a completely different dimension to the visit."

A calling system is most successful if it is designed to meet the needs of both the newcomer and the lay caller. Consideration of both parties involved is important. If possible, assign hospitality ministers to visitors in or near their own neighborhoods, giving them as much available information as possible about the person to be visited. Supplying the caller with a loaf of bread, as well as information about the church to give the newcomer, can also increase the comfort level of both parties.

From the information on the Act of Friendship tablet, the hospitality ministry chairperson can develop a record of all newcomer visits. A sample record-keeping form for this purpose is shown on page 68. In addition to providing information for afternoon visits by hospitality ministers, the friendship tablet can be helpful in a number of other ways. For example, after one visit to Madison Street United Methodist Church in Clarksville, Tennessee, newcomers begin receiving that church's newsletter. "If you breathe, you get our weekly newsletter," stated Bob Irvine, director of music ministries at the church. "It makes a difference when newcomers immediately begin receiving weekly reminders of church events," he said. If a newcomer does not attend for six to eight weeks in a row, the person's name is taken off the mailing list. If the person suddenly comes back, he or she is immediately added to the list once again. After a second visit, Bob telephones newcomers with information about the church's choir program, which serves the needs of people from age five to adult. If the visitors have school-age children, they also receive a call from the director of religious education. Using this system, the church has grown by more than 100 members per year in the last two years.

After a newcomer's third visit, a letter from the clergy can be mailed, along with a form to be returned to the church. See Chapter 4, page 70 for a copy of this Newcomer Information Sheet (Handout 4D). Because it is important for clergy to have personal contact with as many newcomers as possible, a clergy call is also desirable at this time.

In addition, some churches may want to assign a "shepherd" to each newcomer. Shepherds should be parishioners who know their way around the congregation and are willing to shepherd a new member for at least two years. Shepherds can introduce newcomers to as many people as possible and invite them to sit with them at various church functions. Moreover, shepherds may want to call their newcomers once a month just to see how they are doing. Likewise, clergy and/or the hospitality ministry chairperson may want to check in regularly with the shepherds to see if they are comfortable in their role with newcomers.

When hospitality ministers and shepherds are secure in their roles, they often begin to claim the authority which is theirs as lay ministers, thereby fostering a feeling of shared ministry between clergy and laity. Not only are clergy and laity performing similar functions in welcoming the new member, but there is also a feeling of shared ministry with regard to the pastoral care of newcomers. These lay ministers can often share valuable insights about newcomers with clergy, increasing clergy awareness of special areas of need. Meeting the needs of hospitality ministers in their functions as both greeters and callers, as well as the needs of shepherds, is not only critical to the success of a church's hospitality ministry, but is equally important in developing the concept of lay ministry within a parish.[9]

Educating Newcomers about the Church;
Educating the Church about Newcomers

In addition to providing these personal contacts with new
people, effective newcomer programs educate new members
about the parish while simultaneously educating the parish
about new people. Trinity Church in Princeton, New Jersey, successfully uses several different methods for this mutual education. It offers a newcomer forum in the fall, a newcomer party at
the rector's home in the spring, and a monthly article in the
church newsletter. Because people respond to a variety of activities, this church finds it helpful to offer at least two newcomer
events with differing formats throughout the year. Each activity
serves a distinct purpose and meets a variety of needs, therefore
reaching a broad range of people.

The first of these, the Sunday morning newcomer forum, is
led by the laity of Trinity Church. Committee chairpersons give
a brief overview of their particular areas, with most of the time
devoted to a question-and-answer period. A handout describing
church programs is also provided. At such events, it is important
to stress that newcomers do not have to become involved in any
of these activities. The information should not be given for re-
cruitment purposes, but rather to stimulate discussion and questions about various church offerings.

Trinity's newcomer party in the spring is designed to greet
newcomers on a more informal basis. Because this event is not
held on Sunday morning, it attracts additional new people who
attend weekday and early Sunday services.

In planning your own events, make sure that lay leaders attend the party and forum, because it is important to provide an
environment in which the parish as a whole can share the responsibility of welcoming new members. In addition, it is best if
as many parishioners as possible staff the name tag area on
Sunday morning.

Even though these responsibilities are shared, the parish at
large is often unaware of the number of new people who are becoming a part of their worshiping community. To address this
need, Trinity publishes "Newcomer News" in their church
newsletter. In addition to the names and addresses of new members, a paragraph is included that informs the parish about newcomer events, suggests that people call newcomers in their

neighborhoods, or reminds parishioners to be especially aware of new people during the summer months. This consciousness-raising effort is well received, and many parishioners note with surprise the large number of new members.[10]

Events such as these are invaluable tools in helping newcomers feel at home in a large parish; yet this is only the beginning of what it means to be hospitable in the Christian sense. True hospitality within a church setting must reach to the deeper parts of our faith. True integration is not only integration into one church, but integration into the body of Christ. This requires a different kind of education, a deeper sense of community, and a deeper commitment.

All Saints Church in Pasadena, California, has developed a covenant program to address this need. The purpose of the program is to prepare adults for confirmation in the Episcopal Church and for membership in All Saints. A person who decides not to be confirmed may become a general member of All Saints. The difference between this and other new-member incorporation programs is that it has a twofold structure. It is held once a week on nine weeknight evenings from 7:30 p.m. to 9:30 p.m. The first hour is used for a forum presentation; the second hour is for small covenant group meetings. On the Saturday before confirmation, a Quiet Day is held from 8:30 a.m. to 3:00 p.m. with a covenant dinner given at 6:00 p.m.[11]

The small covenant group meetings, held immediately after the forum presentation, focus on spiritual issues and enable participants to know one another on a deeper level. The covenant groups are small and are led by the laity. The importance of such groups cannot be overstated. *Once the initial welcoming is over, there must be a structure designed specifically for new people, enabling them to come together in a more intimate environment.* All Saints' introductory letter to covenant groups describes this focus in greater detail and can be found on page 75.

As the strangers we welcome on Sunday morning become active members of our congregations, it is important that we not assume that they are well integrated after the first year. In a large church, the one-year anniversary for a newcomer is a critical one. For this reason, it is best if newcomers can be contacted by a member of the clergy or by the hospitality ministry chairperson at the one-year mark.

Newcomer Programs in the Small Church

In family- and pastoral-size churches, a conscious effort on be-
half of newcomers is still necessary, although it need not be as
elaborate as that in program and corporation churches. For example, the dynamics are quite different in a family church. To
implement a hospitality ministry effectively in this setting, it is
important to understand what those dynamics are. Family
churches with fifty members or fewer often operate as a single-
cell unit that can be "so warm you can't get in."[12] In churches of
this size, there is generally one person who introduces new people to parish leaders. Newcomers are often screened in this way
and then adopted one-by-one into the church family.

In a family church, spiritual formation of the key welcomers is
necessary to fostering Christian openness. They need to be conscious of their role in welcoming new members. They need to be
sensitive about filling in the newcomer on what people are talking and laughing about. They need to be aware that in the powerful desire of some churches to stay small, there can be a kind of
cruel homogeneity that can be less than welcoming. Without
such a spiritual awareness, lay leaders of family churches may ex-
clude people without being aware of the dynamics at play.

Clergy of family parishes interested in building up the membership of their churches might keep in mind that the movement from family to pastoral-size congregations is the most
difficult one to make. Those attached to the single-cell dynamic
of a family parish are there because they like it that way.
Powerful emotions and language can follow even an expressed
desire for growth.

In addition, the expectation in churches of this size is often
that the clergyperson function more as a chaplain rather than as
a trainer for ministry. Thus, training of the laity for newcomer
ministry should begin with education for the parish about the
importance of their role in hospitality ministry.

Another factor to consider is that codependent relationships
can develop between clergy and laity. For a thorough discussion
of this aspect of congregational family systems, see *Generation to
Generation* by Edwin H. Friedman, pages 195-219.

Thus, a newcomer strategy in family parishes is to educate the
laity about their role in welcoming new members, to attend to
the spiritual formation of the key welcomers, to replace them if

necessary after prayerful consideration, to add new helpers as growth requires, and to be aware of possible codependent relationships between clergy and laity.

In pastoral-size parishes, most of the basic elements of the program outlined here can be implemented. Training programs should be designed using the workshop outlined in Chapter 5. The material can be tailored to meet the needs of your individual parish.

A hospitality ministry chairperson is needed in pastoral congregations to handle the administrative duties. However, a structured hospitality committee is not necessary. Instead, a more flexible strategy is best, with the clergy assuming a central role and selecting about three to four helpers, based on their gifts for a newcomer ministry. Rather than a structured committee, it is best to think of this group as a team.

Use of an Act of Friendship tablet is not necessary in family or pastoral churches. Visitors are easier to spot, and names can be obtained by a hospitality minister at the door before and after the service. Moreover, one newcomer event per year is usually adequate.

Regardless of size, every church that undertakes a hospitality ministry needs to be clear about the ultimate goal of such ministry. The goal is for newcomers to become Christ's conscious agents in the setting of their daily lives—at work, at home, in the community, in the area of citizenship, in leisure activities—as well as within the church. *Without this vision for mission in the world, a church's hospitality program can be centered inward toward the needs of the individual congregation, rather than outward toward the needs of the world.* Success is most likely if this vision is at the heart of a church's hospitality program and is articulated throughout its development.

The prophet Isaiah tells us, "Enlarge the site of your tent, and let the curtains of your habitations be stretched out; do not hold back; lengthen your cords and strengthen your stakes" (Is 54:2). For churches who want to "enlarge the site of their tent," an effective hospitality program must be in place. For parishioners to "not hold back," consciousness raising and education are needed concerning our call as Christians to hospitality ministry. As we "lengthen our cords" and "strengthen our stakes," it is we who will be strengthened and enriched, both as a church and as individuals. For it is "through the stranger our view of self, of world, of God is deepened and expanded. Through the stranger we are given a chance to find ourselves. And through the stranger, God finds us and offers us the gift of wholeness."[13]

Chapter 4

FORMS FOR IMPLEMENTING THE PROGRAM

As lay leaders begin to assume the authority that is theirs, they will need concrete tools for implementing and running lay ministry programs in their church. Establishing a successful newcomer program takes not only the knowledge of what should be included, but numerous forms to put the program into effect. Since their development can be time-consuming, forms are provided here that have been successfully used to implement the program described in Chapter 3. Please refer to Chapter 3 for additional information as you use these forms in developing your own program.

All of the forms are generic. Therefore, they can be typed on your own letterhead and used as is. However, you may want to personalize them to reflect your particular church. Each form has been numbered for purposes of clarification and should be used as handouts in your workshop presentation.

The sample forms and letters in this chapter are designed to be used in the following ways:

4A — ACT OF FRIENDSHIP TABLET.
See Chapter 3, page 57, for an explanation of this form.

4B — NEWCOMER HISTORY.
See Chapter 3, page 58 for an explanation of this form.

4C — WELCOMING LETTER.
Mail with 4D and 4E after third visit.

4D — NEWCOMER INFORMATION SHEET.
Mail with 4C and 4E after third visit.

4E — BROCHURE. Forms 4C, 4D, and 4E are mailed together
following the third visit, along with an envelope addressed to the church. The letter should be signed by the
clergy.

4F — NEWCOMER FORUM INVITATION. This can be a
simple postcard giving the necessary information. It
should be signed by the person leading the forum. Your
newcomer party invitation should be designed by you to
fit the party planned. For this reason, it is not included
here. Both invitations should be mailed three weeks before the event. Be sure also to include several announcements in your church newsletter and Sunday leaflet.

4G — NEWCOMER NEWS should be printed monthly in
your church newsletter and can contain the type of information found in this sample.

4H — INTRODUCTION TO COVENANT GROUPS. This
notice should be given out at the first covenant group
meeting. See Chapter 3, page 61 for an explanation for
these meetings.This form was developed by All Saints
Church, Pasadena, California, and is used with permission.

4I — REQUEST FOR LETTER OF TRANSFER. This form
should be distributed at a covenant group meeting.

ACT OF FRIENDSHIP TABLET

Date: _____

"You shall love the Lord your God with all your heart . . . and your neighbor as yourself (Lk 10:27)." These words of Jesus Christ are the setting for our worship. But sometimes we forget to love those who worship with us. Take time to get to know the people beside you; sign this pad and pass it to others in your pew.

Worshiper (Regular members need only give their names and check "member.")	Member	Visitor	New Resident	Other	Desire Membership Information	Telephone
Name (Ms., Mrs., Mr.)						Home
Address, Zip						Work
Name (Ms., Mrs., Mr.)						Home
Address, Zip						Work
Name (Ms., Mrs., Mr.)						Home
Address, Zip						Work
Name (Ms., Mrs., Mr.)						Home
Address, Zip						Work
Name (Ms., Mrs., Mr.)						Home
Address, Zip						Work
Name (Ms., Mrs., Mr.)						Home
Address, Zip						Work
Name (Ms., Mrs., Mr.)						Home
Address, Zip						Work

HANDOUT 4A

NEWCOMER HISTORY

Name: _____

Address: _____

City, State, Zip: _____

Phone: _____

Comments:

1. First visit   _____

2. Hospitality minister   _____

3. Second visit   _____

4. Third visit   _____

5. Letter and information sheet sent   _____

6. Information sheet returned and   _____
    given to clergy for follow-up

7. Shepherd assigned   _____

8. Further visits   _____

9. Covenant program   _____
    information sent

10. Date of one-year anniversary visit made _____

WELCOMING LETTER

Dear

We are pleased you have begun to worship with us and hope that in your time here you have experienced some of the joy of God's love that brings us together each week.

The enclosed leaflet will give you a sense of our life as a Christian community. In addition, in the entrance to the church you will find the latest copy of our church news bulletin. It will inform you of our current programs and activities; we sincerely hope you will feel free to participate in those that interest you.

Within the near future, one of our parishioners would like to call you. Before the call assignment is made, it would be helpful if you could complete the enclosed form and return it to us in the self-addressed envelope.

We are delighted that you are worshiping with us and look forward to getting to know you. If you would like more information about our church or if there are any pastoral needs in which I can assist you, please call me.

NEWCOMER INFORMATION SHEET

Name(s) _____ Date _____

Address _____

_____

Phone _____ Best Time to Phone _____

Time of Church Service Usually Attended _____

LIST THE NAME AND DATE OF BIRTH FOR EACH FAMILY MEMBER.
IF YOU HAVE CHILDREN, PLEASE LIST SCHOOL OR COLLEGE AND
CURRENT GRADE LEVEL.

I WOULD LIKE INFORMATION ABOUT:

__ Acolytes   __ Confirmation

__ Altar Guild   __ Outreach Programs

__ Baptism   __ Pastoral Services

__ Choirs   __ Ushers Guild

__ Church School   __ Youth Group

HANDOUT 4D

IN THIS SPACE, PLEASE GIVE US ANY OTHER INFORMATION YOU
WOULD LIKE OUR CLERGY TO KNOW.

FOR OFFICE USE ONLY

HANDOUT 4D

Welcome

The people and clergy of Trinity Church welcome you into our community. We hope you will find spiritual nourishment and companionship with us as you seek a new church home.

As Episcopalians we look to scripture, tradition, reason and experience as authority for our faith and worship. These provide a framework for understanding ourselves and our salvation and the way we are meant to live in relationship to God and one another. Our life of worship is centered in the Holy Eucharist, and we encourage you to join us in receiving communion.

*I*n addition to Sunday morning worship and Adult Education Forums, there are smaller weekday services, coffee and fellowship times, study and prayer groups, choirs, and active Church School and Youth Fellowship programs. As prayer and reflection lead us to action, there are

many opportunities for service to those within the parish and beyond who are in need of help.

*T*rinity Church, Princeton, is an Episcopal church in the American branch of the world-wide Anglican Communion. We have deep historic roots and also a willingness to open ourselves to the issues of the contemporary world.

*W*e hope that the moment will come when you will want to become a member of Trinity, to move beyond companionship to commitment. What follows in this pamphlet is intended to help you do that. In the meantime, we encourage you to enter into our life as fully as you can. If you have filled out the Welcome Tablet, our newcomer liaison will be in touch with you soon. We are all on a journey of faith, and we welcome you, whatever your convictions, doubts and hopes.

Photos taken of the Trinity Homecoming Picnic

HANDOUT 4E

Becoming a Member

As Christians we are always growing in faith.

You may be someone who. . .

• seeks baptism.

• is not an Episcopalian and desires Confirmation or to be Received into the Episcopal Church.

• is new in the community and wishes to transfer membership.

• has a child in our Church School or choir and who wishes to know more about our liturgy and Prayer Book.

• is a member of long-standing in the Episcopal Church who seeks to refresh your knowledge.

We want you to become a member. When you are ready to take that step, make an appointment with one of the clergy to discuss your particular concern. The clergy look forward to meeting with you and becoming better acquainted.

Membership classes at Trinity are for newcomers, but also for those who are not new in our midst but may want more adult education about being an Episcopalian. "The Episcopal Church: A Personal Investigation" is the name of our series of classes taught by clergy and laity. These classes give an Anglican perspective on the meaning of our Baptismal vows, Confirmation commitment, and our continual reaffirmation of faith.

As a Member We Ask You. . .

• to be faithful in Sunday worship, realizing that celebrating the Eucharist together is essential to our life as the Body of Christ.

• to be dedicated in service, supporting with time and effort the ministries of Trinity. Here is one of the important ways we gain our personal experience of God; through service we meet Christ in others.

• to be responsible in pledging, conscientious in financial support of the Church. This gives meaning to our prayer in the Eucharist that we "may honor you with our substance and be faithful stewards of your bounty."

Trinity Parish was

founded in 1833. In the colonial period, it was a preaching station of the Trenton mission. The current church, built in 1868, was designed by Richard Upjohn, who designed Trinity, Wall Street, New York, and other historic buildings in the Gothic Revival style. The church on Mercer Street was modified by the architect Ralph Adams Cram, designer of the Princeton University Chapel. The gallery organ was built on classic French design principles by Casavant Freres, Limitee, Quebec, in 1978.

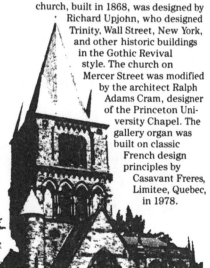

Welcome

We want you to feel at home with us, and we hope you have a sense of expectancy and joy as you join our community at Trinity.

HANDOUT 4E

NEWCOMER FORUM INVITATION

All newcomers are invited to a special Newcomer Forum on
_____ at _____. Our Christian education, worship
and music programs, and pastoral and outreach ministries will be
discussed.

Please join us for a brief presentation, a question and answer
period, and fellowship. I hope to see you there!

HANDOUT 4F

NEWCOMER NEWS

Several parishioners have recently volunteered their services to
our Newcomer Program. _____ and _____
will be co-chairing the name tag table during forum time;
_____ will be working on the newcomer party. Please
call any of us with your ideas, suggestion, or comments. In
addition, ___ parishioners made newcomer calls last year!

Welcoming new people is a responsibility we all share. Please
look out for the many new people who will be joining us over
summer. Since most activities break during July and August, this
is an especially difficult time for new people. We welcome the
following people into the life of our church family.

(Name, children's names and ages, address, and telephone
number should be listed here.)

HANDOUT 4G

INTRODUCTION TO COVENANT GROUPS

Christianity is relentlessly *corporate*. That means that God calls individuals together in the church to discover their *unity* of spirit in spite of their diversity. This is the way Jesus worked with his disciples. People with differing gifts, personalities, backgrounds, and needs are all brought together in the body of Christ. It is a continuing miracle.

The small groups in our covenant program are not just discussion groups; they are little churches-in-formation. You will share your insights and experiences in order that to some degree you may be obedient to Jesus' command: "Bear one another's burdens." In your groups you are not just *talking about* the church, you are *being* the church; not just talking about Christ, but becoming the body of Christ.

Each covenant group has a convener, a member of our church who will be your companion during the course of the program. He or she is not a teacher or leader, but a growing Christian like you whose job it is to help your group accomplish its tasks while sharing fully with you in your journey.

Prayer will be part of your group's experience: brief, simple, spontaneous, and honest. Christian communities live on prayer as surely as they live on the air they breathe. Please enter into your group experience trusting the Spirit of God to guide you, trusting the Spirit of God who is "the Lord and Giver of Life" in the church.

Your faithful attendance is essential. Your group's experience will be diminished by any absences. But if you are sick and cannot attend, please call your leader so your group can keep you in its prayers.

God bless you on your journey.

HANDOUT 4H

REQUEST FOR LETTER OF TRANSFER

To the Rector or Minister in charge of _____

_____
Address

This is to request a Letter of Transfer for:

_____

     Children: _____

           _____

           _____

           _____

(It would be appreciated if you would include pertinent dates, i.e., Birth, Baptism, Confirmation.)

Thank you.

     Signed: _____

           _____

           _____
                 Address

Please mail the completed Letter of Transfer directly to the parish from which the request is being made. It should be returned to our church office at the above address.

Chapter 5

HOSPITALITY MINISTRY WORKSHOP

An imaginative, effective introduction of this hospitality program in your church is critical to promoting parish owner-ship and involvement. Beginning with a sound theological basis for hospitality ministry, this workshop gives parishioners the biblical foundation for extending hospitality to the stranger. Then, the sessions on developing their own hospitality program give them the practical tools they need to put that theology into practice.

In using this workshop, some simple guidelines need to be fol-lowed. First, ask participants to wear name tags during all ses-sions, to emphasize the importance of wearing them on Sunday mornings and at other parish gatherings. Second, *the quotation printed at the beginning of each session should be written on newsprint and placed in a visible location for all to see as they enter the room.* Third, at the first session, give each participant a folder for handouts, as well as an agenda with dates filled in. At subse-quent sessions, give out an agenda for that meeting along with the appropriate handouts.

This workshop can be used in several different formats. The first three sessions serve as excellent consciousness-raising ma-terial for the entire church. Every member of the church needs to be educated about hospitality ministry. Otherwise, the ten-dency is to assume that the hospitality committee is fulfilling this part of the church's responsibility. The importance of own-ership of the program by everyone cannot be overstated. The last three sessions are designed for a small group of parishioners who are interested in developing a hospitality program for the church. In addition, Session 1 can be used to introduce the concept of reaching out to those with specific needs and inter-

77

ests. Each session is designed to last 1 to 1½ hours and can be adapted to meet your particular needs.

If you do not already have in mind a lay chairperson or cochairpersons to head your hospitality committee, note at the first two sessions anyone who seems to be taking a leadership role. This person may be a natural choice. It is important to have a chairperson in place by the end of Session 5, because she or he will lead Session 6.

AGENDA

SESSION 1 (DATE)
Hospitality to All Strangers

SESSION 2 (DATE)
Christ in the Stranger's Guise

SESSION 3 (DATE)
"The Woman in the Red Hat—Why Do You Suppose She's in Church?"

SESSION 4 (DATE)
Components of Successful Hospitality Programs

SESSION 5 (DATE)
Components of Hospitality Programs, Continued: Where Do I Fit In?

SESSION 6 (DATE)
Putting It All Together

Session 1
Hospitality To All Strangers

Materials Needed: Newsprint and marker
Handouts: "Lines To Starlings On A Snowy Day,"
                      page 25.
Quotation: "You know the heart of a stranger, for
                      you were strangers in the land of Egypt"
                      (Ex 23:9, RSV).

1. Begin by reading the quotation printed above, in which God speaks to the Israelites on their exodus journey. Next, make the point that at some time in our lives each of us is the stranger; elaborate using the information found at the beginning of Chapter 1. Then ask, "When you were the stranger, what was in your heart? Who welcomed you and what did they do?" Give participants time to reflect on these questions; then ask each in turn to answer after giving his or her name.

2. Discuss the Judeo-Christian roots of hospitality, as discussed on pages 20-21.

3. Tell the story of the Whoopi Goldberg character in the movie *Sister Act*, as related on pages 22-24. Then give out copies of the poem, "Lines to Starlings on a Snowy Day." Have one of the participants read it aloud; then ask the following questions: "Who are the starlings in your life? Give some examples of possible 'starlings' from page 25 and add your own." Have each participant share her or his thoughts with one other person in the group. Then give everyone a chance to present this information to the group as a whole. Write the answers on newsprint.

4. Give examples of how Jesus "fed the starlings lovingly," as given on pages 26-27. Stress that the distinctiveness of the Christian call to hospitality is in welcoming those who may be unwelcome in other settings. Then ask the following question:
"Can you think of anyone whom you would find difficult to 'feed lovingly,' should that person walk in the doors of your church?"

Session 2
Christ in the Stranger's Guise

Materials Needed:	Newsprint and marker, a Bible, paper and pen for each participant
Handouts:	2C—"Rune of Hospitality," page 49. 2D—*Christ Appearing as a Gardener to Mary Magdalene*, page 50.
Quotation:	"I was a stranger and you welcomed me" (Mt 25:35b).

1. Explore guest/host reversals in light of the discussion on pages 28-30, focusing on the stories of Sarah and Abraham and the three heavenly strangers, and Jesus and the strangers on the road to Emmaus.

2. Ask a participant to read aloud the "Rune of Hospitality" and then give a copy to each of the participants for their folders, stressing the centrality of this message in the Christian call to welcome the stranger. Read the quotation from Matthew 25 aloud, printed above.

3. How do we receive the Christ in the stranger's guise? First of all, by listening. Read aloud the following quotation from *The Listener*, by Taylor Caldwell: "The most desperate need of people today is not . . . a new religion, or a new 'way of life.' . . . People's real need, their most terrible need, is for someone to listen to them, not as a 'patient,' but as a human soul. They need to tell someone of what they think, of the bewilderment they encounter when they try to discover why they were born, how they must live, and where their destiny lies."[1] Next, ask participants to think of a time in their lives when they felt they were really being listened to. What did the listener do? How did they feel when responded to in this way? Solicit answers from the group and write them on newsprint.

4. Tell the story of the Host in *The Canterbury Tales*, as presented on page 34. To welcome others in the name of Christ, we need to be good story-listeners, not storytellers. As we listen to others, we need to engage in mutual listening for the word of God revealed to us through the stranger. See page 45 for more information on mutual listening.

5. As we become good story-listeners, we will at some point want to share our lives with those whom God sends our way. Help parishioners focus on what it means to "share the life" both as individuals and as a church. Begin by reading the following passage aloud:

> A faith-centered community, where the pastoral leadership is warm and caring, where the worship life offers quality extra-dependence, and people genuinely support and care for each other, offers something unavailable anywhere else. These churches have the gift of life, and they need to be taught to share this gift more freely with the seeking, hurting people who wander in their front door. Yet, often the members are so absorbed with drinking at and maintaining the fountain, that they fail to move over so that others can have some of this life-giving water.[2]

What we as a church have to share is this gift of life that has been freely given to each one of us by God—and to each and every person who cares enough to take the time to walk in our door and sit in our pew. Newcomer programs at their heart are about sharing this life, this community, your life, your community.

6. How can a parish successfully "share the life"? On two levels, both individually and corporately. Individually, we are each unique and God has given each one of us gifts to share. Read 1 Corinthians 12:4-11 aloud. Encourage participants to reflect on the gifts God has given them that they might share with others. You may want to offer to help them individually with their discernment process if they are unclear about their particular gifts. It is best not to explore their individual gifts within the workshop setting since it is a time-consuming process that can divert energy from your primary focus.

Corporately, your parish has much to share with the newcomer. Give each participant a piece of paper and a pen. Ask group members to reflect for a minute on what it is they like about your church. Have them write down what they believe the strengths of your parish are now, and then what they could be in the future. Invite each participant to read her or his list aloud. Write the group's comments on newsprint. Before the next session, type them and provide a photocopy for each participant.

Session 3
"The Woman in the Red Hat—Why Do You Suppose
She's in Church?"

Materials Needed:	Newsprint and marker
Handouts:	5A and 5B
	Photocopies of the list of parish
	strengths developed in Session 2
Quotation:	"Contribute to the needs of the saints;
	extend hospitality to strangers" (Rom
	12:13).

1. Begin by giving out the list of strengths composed by participants at the last gathering. Read several aloud as you remind them that they have a great deal to share as a parish.

2. Read the quotation aloud. State that today's session will focus on the variety of needs that bring newcomers to church.

The woman in the red hat—why do you suppose she's in church? This question is a good one to raise when developing a hospitality program. Why have new people decided to worship here? What do they seek? Give out your own version of "Newcomer Scenarios," or use Handout 5A provided here. Have different parishioners read them aloud one at a time. After each, discuss the needs of the newcomer described.

3. Ask participants to reflect for a moment on what they seek from the church. Why do they set their alarms on Sunday morning for church rather than sleeping late or reading the Sunday paper? Have participants share their reflections in groups of two for five minutes. Then present the findings to the group as a whole. Write these reflections on newsprint.

4. It is helpful to tell participants that newcomers' reasons for seeking the church are often similar to their own. Research has shown that people most often seek the church for (a) refreshment, support, growth and fulfillment, faith and fellowship; (b) their family, help in raising children, keeping relationships together; and (c) for a sense of belonging. In addition, many reported a significant change in their lives that preceded their reinvolvement with church life. Generally, people do not seek the church during a crisis. Instead, their reinvolvement is connected with the restructuring and reordering of their lives after

the crisis.[4] State that everyone experiences the universal life events of birth, death, illness and, possibly, moving, changing jobs, or new responsibilities at work. Such life experiences, common to us all, may bring a person to seek the church.[5] Thus, each participant will have unique gifts to share with the newcomer—gifts that no one else can or will share in quite the same way.

5. To close this session, distribute Handout 5B, "Hello, I Am a Newcomer to Your Church," to the participants.[6] Ask one of them to read it aloud to the group. (This is also an excellent reflective piece to print in your parish newsletter as you introduce your newcomer program to the parish at large.)

Session 4
Components of Successful Hospitality Programs

Materials Needed:	Newsprint and markers
Handouts:	4A through 4E (included in Chapter 4) 5C
Quotation:	"Enlarge the site of your tent, and let the curtains of your habitations be stretched out; do not hold back; lengthen your cords and strengthen your stakes" (Is 54:2).

1. Begin by saying that to "enlarge the site of our tents" and to "stretch out our curtains" today requires a comprehensive hospitality program for attracting, inviting, greeting, calling, orienting, and incorporating new members. In establishing such a program, it is important to state at the outset that the goal of hospitality programs is for newcomers to become Christ's conscious agents in the settings of their daily lives—at work, at home, in the community, in the area of citizenship, in leisure activities, as well as within the church. Without this vision for mission in the world, a church's hospitality program can be centered inward toward the needs of the individual congregation, rather than outward toward the needs of the world. This outward vision is foundational to a sound hospitality program and should be articulated throughout the remaining workshop sessions.

Next, participants should be urged to begin thinking about which part of the program they might want to work on further. *After each of the following sections, have them brainstorm ways they might implement that segment of the program in their church.* Write their ideas on newsprint and save it. In this introductory workshop, it is helpful to give participants more ideas than they can use. This gives them the freedom to put together their own program, which will promote group ownership of the project.

2. If your church has decided to implement one of the programs outlined in chapters 6 and 7, that fact should be mentioned here. If you are unclear about such programming, just mention that one way to attract new members to the church is through innovative programming geared to groups with special needs—the bereaved or the poor, for example—or to a group with special interests, such as the business community.

3. Present the information included in sections 3a-3c to participants in lecture format.

a. Lutheran Church historian Martin Marty says that one word defines the difference between churches that grow and those that don't: *invite.* Marty reports a study that indicates that the average Episcopalian invites someone to church once every twenty-eight years. His statistic may be an exaggeration, but his point is not. When a church isn't growing, its members are not "inviting."[7]

Research has shown that three out of four previously unchurched persons were influenced by a friend or family member to come to church. The body of Christ grows person-by-person, family-by-family, through a lay person who cares enough about a friend, neighbor, colleague, or family member to offer her or him a bridge to relationship with Christ and his church. If the invitation does not begin with loving concern, it will not succeed.[8]

One way to encourage inviting is by scheduling a "Bring a Friend Sunday" in your church. This method has been used by hundreds of congregations during the last five years. A pastor in Mulvane, Kansas, says, "In five years, we have had a total of 275 visitors to worship at our five Bring-a-Friend Sundays. Many of these persons subsequently joined our church."[9]

It is important to stress that the invitation is always God's, not ours nor our church's.[10] Invitations should be extended only after prayful consideration by the person doing the inviting.

A fast-growing United Methodist church in Richland, Washington, has used the following method twice a year for several years. A few weeks before Christmas and Easter, the pastor schedules five minutes of meditative background music in the morning worship service. After the ushers distribute 3- by 5-inch cards, the pastor asks worshipers to write down the names of everyone they can think of who does not attend church. He then asks them to pray for those people every day for the next two weeks. During morning worship two weeks later, he urges worshipers to invite to church those people for whom they have been praying. Average worship attendance has grown from three hundred to twelve hundred during the past dozen years.[11]

b. Contacting people who have recently moved into your area is another way to reach out beyond the walls of your church. Since people new to your community are in a transition period, they are often receptive to a church's welcoming invitation.

c. Using printed material to "advertise" can reach large numbers of people with minimal expense. Articles about parish activities should be sent to the local newspapers. A brochure about the parish, such as the sample included on pages 72-73, can be mailed out to people in a targeted area. Moreover, such brochures are valuable simply left in the narthex of the church or on a tract rack for newcomers to take. In some churches a community newsletter has been an effective way to reach people who live near the church. The emphasis here is on the parish's role as neighbor. Offerings at the church that might be of interest in the community should also be highlighted, such as church school and adult education events, guest speakers, inquirers classes, Bible study, and concerts.[12] In addition, a well-publicized, well-run vacation church school can provide outreach to young families.

d. Reflecting on the appearance of the church facility can help parishioners see their church in a new light. Instruct participants to shut their eyes and picture themselves approaching their church with no previous knowledge of it. What do they see? Are there signs out front that are clearly visible from the road? What is the general condition of the church? Does it look inviting, welcoming? If not, what can easily be changed?

Next, have them imagine what it would be like to walk into the church building for the first time. Are areas clearly marked with attractive, permanent signs? For example, would newcomers know where to find the nursery, church school, parish hall, rest rooms, church offices? Is the interior of the church well maintained? Do the walls need a new coat of paint? Do the floors need to be professionally waxed? *First impressions count.* We tell visitors much about our church by both interior and exterior appearance.

e. Is there a tract rack in your church? If not, discuss the possibility of obtaining one. If there is a tract rack, discuss its location. Is it visible to everyone who comes in your church? Is there a rack in more than one location? Does it contain information about your denomination and your particular church? Is the tract rack kept full at all times?

4. a. In your discussion of recognizing and greeting newcomers, pass out a photocopy of the cartoon on Handout 5C which highlights a concern shared by many parishioners as they consider extending hospitality to the stranger.[13] This cartoon, which could be called "The Attack of the Killer Greeters," should be discussed in terms of balance. Whereas parishioners should not ignore new people, neither should they bombard them with greetings.

Another frequent concern of parishioners when making an effort to welcome newcomers is that the person they believe is a newcomer may actually be a member of long-standing. The awkwardness of this situation can be prevented by simply saying to the person, "I don't believe I've met you. I'm _____." Regardless of how long a person may have been attending the church, if he or she is new to you, you should make an effort to meet that person.

b. Discuss the role of hospitality ministers as greeters on Sunday morning, as discussed on page 54.

c. Distribute Handouts 4A and 4B, the "Act of Friendship tablet"[14] and "Newcomer History." Discuss their use in light of the material on pages 57-59.

d. Discuss the use of name tags during adult education events and coffee hour as related on page 56.

Session 5
Components of Hospitality Programs, Continued—
Where Do I Fit In?

Materials Needed:	Newsprint and marker
Handouts:	2C (included in Chapter 2).
	4F, 4G, 4H and 4I(included in
	Chapter 4).
Quotation:	"Let mutual love continue. Do not ne-
	glect to show hospitality to strangers, for
	by doing that some have entertained an-
	gels without knowing it" (Heb 13:1-2).

1. Begin by having the group sing "Angels" (handout 2C, page 47) together. If possible arrange for guitar accompaniment or play the song on a cassette, which can be ordered (see page 48 for details).

2. Read aloud the following story from Herb Miller's *How to Build a Magnetic Church:*

The pastor was astonished at his welcome. He had just arrived at an ancient Coptic monastery out in the desert, nearly a day's journey from Cairo, Egypt. The monks treated him as if he were the one important guest they had been awaiting since the place was established in the twelfth century. They served a fine meal, showed him to a comfortable room, and brought him a bouquet of flowers. He was then greeted by the abbot of the monastery, Father Jeremiah.

"Wow!" said the pastor. "You sure know how to treat visitors."

Father Jeremiah replied, "We always treat guests as if they were angels, just to be safe."[15]

State that this Coptic monastery had put into practice the words from Hebrews in today's quotation; then read the quotation aloud. Comment on the number of angels in their community that may be unknown to participants at this time—angels who are waiting to be welcomed and visited by them.

3. a. The lay calling system enables us to visit God's many angels and is the cornerstone of any hospitality program. First, discuss the concept of hospitality ministers as both Sunday morning greeters and Sunday afternoon callers. See page 57 for details of this program. Be sure to stress the research findings on calling

the day of a person's first visit, and on lay calls versus clergy calls for the initial visit.

b. After describing the program, ask participants how they would feel about making a call. Address any concerns they may have.

4. Orienting both newcomers and parishioners is the first step in the important process of integration. New members can be educated by covenant groups, a newcomer forum, and a newcomer party, as well as through contact with their "shepherds" and other parishioners. Distribute copies of Handout 4F discussing the type of newcomer party and forum your parish might host.

The parish is educated through parishwide newcomer events, rotation of coffee hour greeters and name tag table hosts, and through "Newcomer News." Discuss the sample "Newcomer News" on Handout 4G.

A bulletin board in the parish hall can serve as a pictorial directory for parishioners and newcomers alike. Snapshots, regularly updated, of older and newer members with their names posted below can be fun for everyone as well as helpful. Pictures of various church groups can serve as an additional guide for new people.

5. Integration into the congregation can be one of the most difficult stages for newcomers. Once the initial welcomes are over, there must be a structured system in place to enable newcomers to come together and know each other in a more intimate environment. For this purpose, the covenant group program[16] is superb. Tell about this new member incorporation program, discussed on pages 54-60, and give out copies of Handouts 4H and 4I.

At the end of this session, ask each person to sign up for the part of the program she or he wishes to work on further. Write group members' selections on newsprint. Participants should be prepared to make recommendations to the group in two weeks on the portions of the program they have chosen to use in their church. As participants leave, give them the newsprint with brainstorming ideas for their particular sections.

Session 6
Putting It All Together

Materials Needed: Newsprint and marker
Handouts: None
Quotation: "Listen! I am standing at the door, knocking; if you hear my voice and open the door, I will come in to you and eat with you, and you with me" (Rev 3:20).

1. Begin by reading the quotation aloud. Talk of the excitement of finally getting to the point of putting your own hospitality program together, stressing the many gifts and surprises that await those who welcome the Christ in the stranger's guise.

2. Discuss and decide how the overall program will be put together and implemented. Go around the room and have each person share what they have decided with the group. This session should be led by the new hospitality chairperson.

The number and date of future gatherings should be decided upon by the hospitality committee.

After this session, type up each section heading with the name of the person responsible for it, along with the ideas that will be put into effect. Mail it to each participant along with the biggest thank you imaginable for their time and effort!

NEWCOMER SCENARIOS

1. I've just moved here with my husband and new baby. I started a part-time job last week to help out with our bills. With a new baby, a new job, and a new community to get acquainted with, I feel pulled in several directions at once. I've been to your church four times.

2. I'm single and I live 1,000 miles from my parents, brothers, and sisters. I have no family nearby so I'm looking for a church family. My job is taking up more and more of my time, and I'm finding it difficult to have much of a social life. I moved here two years ago but just began seeking a church home last month.

3. I stopped going to church for a while, but I just feel that I want to come back right now. I feel peaceful here, even though it's different from my former church home. It's strange, yet somehow familiar to me. I don't want to join a committee now. I've done all of that. I just want to feel the peace of the worship services. My mother died last year and I feel better after church—closer to God and, I guess, to my mother in some way.

4. My former parish emphasized my role as a lay minister in my daily life—my work, my home, my community, and my leisure activities, as well as within the church. I need support, encouragement, and continued education about my call to Christ's ministry of work in the world.

5. I have been homeless for four years now and spend most of my time on the streets. It's not a bad way of life, really. I've gotten used to it. The only way I can survive, though, is through my faith. I was walking past this church one Sunday and heard the music. It sounded so beautiful, I decided to come in. I know I don't exactly dress like everyone else, but it's important for me to be here. This place feels like home to me.

HANDOUT 5A

Hello, I Am a Newcomer to Your Church

You cannot know the reason why I am here this morning. It may be as simple as a move to your community or as complicated as personal crisis that leads me to seek strength from God. In either case, I am here. And I will probably remain here and come back to worship with you next Sunday and the Sunday after and the Sunday after that, if you will do some things for me. Won't you please . . .

- Smile at me as I walk in the door. You are my first impression of the church during the first few moments I am in your building, and this first impression will probably stay with me a long time.

- Help me find my place in the service. I will not find your help an intrusion. In fact, I will remember your kindness.

- Speak to me during the coffee hour. I know you want to see your friends and settle that piece of committee business. But I may find it hard to believe that you truly care for each other unless I first see evidence that you care for "the stranger in your midst."

- Tell me good things about your church and your minister. I want to believe that I have come to a place where people love each other and where they believe that they are doing something exciting and important for the Lord.

- Notice me—even if I am not a "family." I don't want to feel invisible just because I am unmarried, a single parent, a teenager, or an older person.

- Talk to me again the second week when I come back, and the third and the fourth. I am still not a part of your parish family. Please don't feel you have "done your duty" by me just because you made a point of greeting me the first week I was here.

- Invite me to become part of some church group or organization. I need more than worship every Sunday. I need to know that I am accepted and affirmed by a group of people within the church who know me by my first name and who care about me as an individual.

HANDOUT 5B

- If you can find it in your heart to do these things for me, I will come back . . . the second Sunday, the third, and maybe forever. I will worship with you, and I may join your choir, work at your fair, teach in your church school, contribute to your canvas, and become a highly involved member of your church, and, in so doing, I will find my own life immeasurably enriched.

Written by the Rev. Christopher Chamberlin Moore, Director of Communication, Episcopal Diocese of New Jersey, and used here with permission.

HANDOUT 5B (continued)

The Last Pew by Heuss

PART III

Chapter 6

OUTREACH TO THE BEREAVED; OUTREACH TO THE POOR

Once an effective newcomer system is in place to meet the needs of the many strangers who find their way to your church, it is important to consider taking the next step. Just as we are called to offer our church home to those who find their way to us, it is equally important to reach out actively beyond the walls of our own church. Why? "Churches and Church Membership in the United States 1990," a county-by-county study of religious membership in our country "proves conclusively that, in most parts of the East and Midwest, 25 percent to 50 percent of the population has no religious affiliation. From the eastern borders of Montana, Wyoming, Colorado and New Mexico to the Pacific, that number increases dramatically to above 75 percent in many areas."[1] What greater stimulus can there be for actively seeking out the many unchurched people in our own communities? Numerous books have been written about reaching out to people as individuals, to bring them into the body of Christ. I would like to offer an alternative to this more individualistic approach, based on the premise that *churches with creative programming geared to meet the needs of specific groups of people will attract new members from those groups.*

Just as reaching out to meet people where they are individually is important, it is equally important to reach out consciously as a church to groups of people, to meet them where they are. Churches considering this type of outreach can reflect on whether there is a particular group of people they feel called to serve and to bring into the body of Christ. For example, God may be calling your congregation to ministry with youth, singles, young families, the elderly, the sick, the unemployed, or the homeless. The possibilities are endless, making clarity of purpose

97

a vital first step for any church actively engaged in this aspect of hospitality ministry.

Creative outreach to particular groups requires creative programming, different from that offered by most churches. To facilitate your own outreach planning, chapters 6 and 7 of this book contain three different programs, geared to ministry with diverse groups of people.

Mother Jones, known as the miner's angel for organizing coal miner's unions, once admonished her nineteenth century followers to "pray for the dead and fight like hell for the living." A poster with her memorable words hangs in my study and has served as an inspiration to me on numerous occasions. "Praying for the dead" and those who mourn them is what the first outreach program described here is all about. "Fighting for the living" is the focus of the other two. The "living" I have chosen to focus on are the poor, and people in the business community. The diversity of people served by these programs is meant to be reflective of the variety of needs within God's created order. This offering is not meant to be exhaustive, but merely suggestive of the type of outreach programming that can be successfully implemented in the church setting.

Outreach to the Bereaved

Reaching out to the stranger who is grieving the loss of a loved one is embedded in the tradition of our faith. The Gospel of John tells us that following the death of Lazarus many neighboring Jews came to Mary and Martha to console them about their brother. When Jesus arrived, he saw these people weeping with their bereaved friends. He was greatly disturbed in spirit and deeply moved. Then Jesus began to weep (Jn 11:18–35).

Providing an opportunity for people to come together to share one another's grief is as central to the healing process now as it was in Jesus' time. Today, such efforts often occur immediately following a death, but the consolation and care end soon after the funeral, just as the real journey of pain is beginning. It is often the case in our fast-paced society that people in bereavement are given the unspoken message that grieving is something to recover from quickly. It often happens that several months following a death, people are no longer asked how they are feeling. The death is seldom mentioned, leaving the bereaved person, who still feels the pain of the loss, feeling isolated and somehow set apart because her or his inner pain is not validated. For this reason, any church that offers well-publicized programs for the bereaved is providing an invaluable service to the community it serves. After the death of a loved one, many people who are lapsed church members or who are unchurched will look to the church for support, but little may be offered, beyond one-on-one support by clergy or a caring parishioner.

To reach out to the bereaved stranger in your midst, it is helpful to begin with a well-publicized adult education event. If possible, ask a local professional in the field to lead the forum. A series such as "Understanding Grief" or "Helping Children Cope with Grief" will attract many within your community who are seeking support. When faced with grieving the loss or impending loss of a loved one, people suddenly find themselves at a place they knew they would be at some point in their lives, but for which few are prepared. The questions, the anger, the hurt, the guilt, and all the other feelings associated with grief rise to the surface with an intensity that can be overwhelming. Reaching out to the stranger in such a time is nothing less than God's call to each one of us as Christian people.

Nevertheless, as a church offers forums on grief, it is helpful to keep in mind that it is a topic our society as a whole often ignores; individuals within our churches will reflect these societal norms. Whereas many will be eager to attend such educational events, others may quite consciously avoid them. It is the pervasive fear of the topic itself that such forums will take steps to alleviate. In addition, they will offer support to those who are grieving and practical suggestions for those who want to help their bereaved sisters and brothers in Christ.

As soon as a parish's adult education events are under way, it is important to offer ongoing support to the bereaved. This offering can be announced at the forums and publicized in the church newsletter and Sunday bulletins, as well as in the community newspaper.

A particularly appropriate worship service for such occasions is the eucharist in which the death and resurrection of Christ are celebrated. The service may be offered quarterly during the week, in conjunction with major baptism days—All Saints', the Baptism of our Lord, Easter, and Pentecost. Because in baptism all die and rise again with Christ, any time of baptismal renewal is a time to remember departed loved ones. At the service, worshipers could be urged to come back on the Lord's day for the baptismal feast. The connection between death and resurrection in both the eucharistic and baptismal rites both underscores an important theological point and encapsulates the healing ministry the church has to offer.

Churches interested in a monthly Eucharist in Remembrance of the Departed would need to select additional occasions for the service. These services could be offered at Lesser Feasts or Commemorations that honor the heavenly birthdays of the saints of our church. It would also be quite appropriate to offer a service on Ascension Day.

In planning your service, you may want to refer to the prayer, scripture, and hymn suggestions included at the end of this chapter on pages 109-113. Churches that feel more comfortable offering a prayer service in remembrance of the departed may also find these suggestions helpful.

It is best to offer the worship service around lunchtime, followed by a light lunch and fellowship. During the service, feelings often rise to the surface, so it is helpful to provide a safe place for people to share those feelings afterward.

During lunch, name tags may be provided, as well as a sign-in sheet for names, addresses, and the name and date of death of the one being remembered. This provides necessary follow-up information. Handwritten notes can be sent to the bereaved three months, six months, one year, and two years following the death, informing them that their loved one will be remembered at the eucharist, or prayer service, that month. This method is pastorally responsible to the needs of the bereaved. It also facilitates the process of ongoing community building. A sample record-keeping form for pastoral follow-up and note writing are included on page 114.

During lunchtime, it is important for some structure to be provided by a facilitator. Without a focused discussion, the gathering can turn into a social occasion. First it is helpful to go around the table, allowing people to introduce themselves and tell about the person for whom they are grieving. Again, story-listening is the way to begin; for in listening to each person, everyone can understand where others are in their process of bereavement. After this, a brief five-minute meditation is all that is needed to get the conversation focused and started.

The best conversation starters are poems written by the bereaved, or excerpts from books in which someone writes of the experience of a loved one's death. People will often identify with what is read, which opens them to share their own feelings and experiences.

At the end of this chapter, I have included several poems that can be read during your lunch gatherings. They were written during my own period of bereavement following the death of my mother, Dorothy Bradley Rankin, on March 20, 1991. They are offered in memory of her.

Books relating a personal grief experience which I recommend for this use are *In Memoriam* and *A Letter of Consolation* by Henri Nouwen, concerning his mother's death; *A Grief Observed* by C.S. Lewis, about his wife's death from cancer; *Lament for a Son* by Nicholas Wolterstorff, concerning his twenty-five-year-old son who was killed in an accident; and *Words I Never Thought to Speak: Stories of Life in the Wake of Suicide* by Victoria Alexander, containing numerous personal accounts of the experience of suicide by a family member. An excellent, all-around resource book is *Hope for Bereaved: Understanding, Coping and Growing Through Grief* by Therese S. Schoeneck. This is a handbook of helpful articles written by bereaved people for other bereaved people and those who want to help them. It can be ordered through Hope for Bereaved, Inc., 4500 Onondaga Boulevard, Syracuse, NY 13219.

Through church programs for the bereaved, old and new parishioners alike often find a common bond through their grieving, much as did those who wept with Mary and Martha following the death of Lazarus. In his book *Power in Weakness*, the Right Rev. Frederick H. Borsch writes: "The power of love which comes to full strength in weakness is different from all other power we experience. . . . Indeed the more that power is shared, the more power there is."[2] In bereavement groups, it has been a joy for me to see the power of love that is shared in the midst of grieving. The more parishioners share that love with others, the more love they have to give. Reaching out to the bereaved stranger and providing a place for this to occur is a gift both to the members of the host church and to the community it is there to serve in the name of Christ.

Outreach to the Poor

Churches considering reaching out to the poor can begin with parishwide education on the biblical basis for doing so. Questions that might be addressed are; What are the theological reasons for such ministry? How do we as Christian people relate to the poor as we offer them community in the body of Christ? Who are the poor?

Throughout the history of Christianity, some scholars have interpreted "the poor" to mean the poor in spirit. Yet such interpretation is not in line with the meaning of the New Testament Greek word for "poor," *ptochos*, which means "one who does not have what is necessary to subsist and is forced into the degrading activity of begging."[3] In *A Theology of Liberation*, Gustavo Gutierrez speaks out against all attempts to transform poverty into spiritual poverty. He writes of "the brute reality of material poverty, [as] lack of sufficient economic goods to lead a full human life, which describes perhaps 70 percent of the human family."[4]

Part of that 70 percent of the human family lives somewhere in your community and mine. Regardless of how affluent a community is, there are nearly always those living below the poverty line nearby. Jesse Jackson's well-known slogan "Think Globally, Act Locally" applies here. It is important to minister to people in developing nations, but if we ignore those in our own backyards, we are missing something.

Before I began my own outreach ministry at Martin House in Trenton, New Jersey, I was reminded of the poor primarily in Sunday morning sermons or weeknight news reports. On such occasions, my mind was filled with images of people of color in inner-city settings, of the rural poor throughout our own country, and of masses of hungry, poverty-stricken people in developing nations. My feelings of compassion and concern for these nameless people were often overshadowed by a sense of my own inability to change anything, leaving me with a sense of frustration and helplessness. But since I was able to extend hospitality to the poor through my work at Martin House, they are no longer an abstraction. The poor are Myrtle, Lamar, Emma, Anna, Scott, and Resa. I know now that the poor are parents who have hopes and dreams that their children will have a better life. They are women and men with specific goals for their own lives, who need help in overcoming the many obstacles encountered in reaching them. The poor are people who share our human condition—the joy, as well as the pain, the relief, as well as the suffering.

Kierkegaard wrote, "Religiousness is suffering, not for its own sake, but suffering through participation in the suffering of the world and the world's anguish." God has offered all of us many different ways in which to participate in the pain and suffering of our neighbors, joining their stories with our own, if only for a moment. But first we must not only see the needs around us, but act on the needs we see. "If a brother or sister is naked and lacks daily food, and one of you says to them, 'Go in peace; keep warm and eat your fill,' and yet you do not supply their bodily needs, what is the good of that? So faith by itself, if it has no works, is dead" (Jas 2:15–17).

Both the Old and New Testaments are filled with further injunctions to help the poor. "If there is among you anyone in need, a member of your community in any of your towns within the land that the LORD your God is giving you, do not be hard-hearted or tight-fisted toward your needy neighbor. . . . Open your hand to the poor and needy neighbor in your land" (Dt 15:7,11). The prophet Jeremiah tells us that this is the way to know God. "He judged the cause of the poor and needy; then it was well. Is not this to know me? says the LORD" (Jer 22:16). Scripture states that the Lord "says," not "asks." In Robert McAfee Brown's *Unexpected News: Reading the Bible with Third World Eyes* he writes: "The form of [this] construction allows only for an affirmative answer. Conclusion: to know God is to do justice and righteousness, to vindicate the poor and the needy."[5] In the Jeremiah passage, the Hebrew word for "poor" is *ani*, which literally means a person who occupies a lowly position and is dependent on those who are higher. The Hebrew word for "needy" is *ebyon*, which means one who is asking from others as a beggar.[6] Here, as in the New Testament, the words definitely do not refer to spiritual poverty.

In addition, reaching out to the poor and the outcast was a hallmark of Jesus' ministry. When he read from the scroll of the prophet Isaiah, he proclaimed that he was anointed by God "to bring good news to the poor" (Lk 4:18). He reasserts this claim when John the Baptist, in prison, sends his disciples to ask Jesus if he is "the one to come." Jesus replies, "Go and tell John what you have seen and heard: the blind receive their sight, the lame walk, the lepers are cleansed, the deaf hear, the dead are raised, the poor have good news brought to them" (Lk 7:22). Moreover, his most famous teaching of all, the Sermon on the Mount, begins with concern for the poor: "Blessed are you who are poor, for yours is the kingdom of God. Blessed are you who are hungry now, for you will be filled" (Lk 6:20–21).

A poignant example of this blessedness is found in *The City of Joy* by Dominique Lapierre. In Calcutta, India, where 300,000 people are stranded on the streets and countless others live in one of 3,000 slum areas, one would think hospitality would be a gift few could afford to give. Yet quite the opposite is true. "In these slums people actually put love and mutual support into practice. They knew how to be tolerant of all creeds and castes, how to give respect to a stranger, how to show charity toward beggars, cripples, lepers, and even the insane. Here the weak were helped, not trampled upon. Orphans were instantly adopted by their neighbors and old people were cared for and revered by their children."[7] Such is the kingdom of God.

This same blessed hospitality was revealed to me while I was leading a Bible study in inner-city Trenton, New Jersey. We had just read Matthew 25, in which Jesus tells the righteous, "I was hungry and you gave me food, I was thirsty and you gave me something to drink" (Mt 25:35). "How simple this gospel message is," I remarked, "yet how hard it is to live it in our daily lives." One of the participants, a woman of color from the impoverished community around us, replied, "I don't think it's difficult at all. When someone knocks on your door and they're hungry, you give them food. If they don't have a place to sleep, you let them sleep on your floor." I suddenly thought of the appeals for the Hunger Fund in my own church, and I realized how far removed I was from those who need my help. The poor do not knock on my door; they are comfortably at arm's length. Sitting face-to-face with this woman, who barely had enough to eat herself, brought me face-to-face with the reality of my protected life.

Not only are those of us who live in suburban communities often isolated from the poor in our middle-class neighborhoods, but church programs for the poor can perpetuate this distance. This type of "arm's-length ministry" with the poor is written of in *Urban Perspectives*, a monthly newsletter by Bob Lupton, a psychologist and lay evangelist in inner-city Atlanta. "Our hearts compel us to care. And so we establish clothes closets and food pantries and benevolence budgets. But these do little more than ensure our protection from entanglement with the poor. . . . We create efficient systems rather than effective relationships. By our one-sided giving we retain control while remaining at arm's length from the recipients. It is an attempt to cure without community. And it is not the gospel!"[8]

Jesus makes it clear that in reaching out to the needy, we are not meant to "cure without community." Rather, we are to invite the poor to table fellowship with us. "When you give a luncheon or a dinner, do not invite your friends or your brothers or your relatives or rich neighbors, in case they may invite you in return, and you would be repaid. But when you give a banquet, invite the poor, the crippled, the lame, and the blind. And you will be blessed, because they cannot repay you, for you will be repaid at the resurrection of the righteous" (Lk 14:12–14). Clearly, Jesus' injunction is to offer community, in addition to food, clothing, and the basic necessities of life.

In discussing such hospitality, Barbara, a seasoned lay minister with the poor, expressed concern about the practicalities involved. "Our church has a food pantry and administers housing funds for the poor," she stated. "Many of those we serve often have serious drug or alcohol problems. Quite frankly, most of us are not equipped to deal with problems of this magnitude." It is important for churches who undertake ministry with poor people not to romanticize them. Indeed, some of the poor have problems with alcohol, drugs, or other dependencies, just as do some members of the host church. Ways of dealing with these and other realities should be discussed prior to undertaking this ministry.

To offer "community with a cure" to the poor in their midst, Grace Church in Plainfield, New Jersey, established an after-school choir program for children ages six through twelve. Applicants were chosen on the basis of financial need. Most participants were from homes of the working poor, who were unable to afford standard after-school programs. Students were picked up after school in a Red Cross van and brought to the church, where they enjoyed one-on-one tutoring and recreation, in addition to the choir instruction.

To establish such programs that enable effective relationships to occur, rather than merely an efficient system to be in place, requires careful, prayerful preparation by a congregation. First, a parishwide adult education event can be offered to introduce the concept "Hospitality to All Strangers." Session 1 of the workshop in Chapter 5 is designed for this purpose. In preparing for this workshop, keep in mind that questions will probably be raised about offering hospitality that embodies a "cure with community." Both the challenges and promises of this ministry can be addressed.

At the close of the workshop, you might want to ask for volunteers who are interested in developing a program for reaching out to the poor in their community. From this group, a team can be formed to conduct a community needs assessment. Because ownership of the program is critical, it is best for the assessment to be conducted by an interested group of laypeople, rather than by a seminarian or an outside consultant. The team members can interview directors of a variety of local agencies such as the YMCA, YWCA, Red Cross, Salvation Army, city or county welfare, local hospitals, food pantries, area churches, area schools, and other local social outreach agencies. The form on page 117 can be used to conduct these interviews.[9]

Once the interviewers determine the kinds of needs that are not currently being met, they can begin to discuss which of those needs their church might be able to address. At this point, the team might consider these questions: What kinds of programs will enable effective relationships to develop? What are our talents and skills? Where are we willing to invest large amounts of our own time and energy? Most important, where is the Spirit leading us as we seek to serve God by making the connection between our faith and our works?

When these questions have been addressed, an outreach proposal can be written and distributed to the parish, outlining several different possibilities for ministry with the poor that will enhance relationship building. Attached to the proposal can be questions for reflection and discussion, to be used at an adult education event or for a special retreat day for interested parishioners.

As your church embarks on this type of ministry, it is important to keep in mind that the purpose is not to serve the needy as clients, as "us" versus "them." Ministry is meant to be *with* the poor, not *to* the poor. This outreach ministry should not be entered into with a paternalistic attitude of superiority, implying that members of the host church have all the answers to give. Quite the opposite is true. In reaching out to the poor, we are not only reaching out to our sisters and brothers in Christ, but to the many gifts they bring with them for us. In a ministry of relationship, regard for other people's vulnerability and delight in their offerings to us presupposes that we perceive them as equals, as people who share our common humanity. This equality of host and stranger results in reciprocal acts of hospitality, where both parties have much to give and to be given, thereby at times reversing the guest/host roles.[10]

As relationships develop, volunteers in the program can be encouraged to invite participants to worship at the host church if they are unchurched or are looking for a new church home. It is important that we, as the body of Christ, welcome others into the body, that they may know the life-giving experience of worship in a community of faith.

In his pamphlet *Stay in the City*, Robert Gallagher includes a quotation by William Temple, adapted for use here: "We need education; but still more we need conversion. We need political progress and social reform; but still more we need redemption. We need peace and security, but still more we need eternal life."[11] Gallagher goes on to state, "We do live by bread and that must be attended to; however, we do not live by bread alone. Both go together. The attempt to do the one without the other is an incomplete understanding of the needs of humanity and the mission of the Church."[12]

In Ann McElligott's *Evangelism with the Poor*, she states that in extending this invitation, it is best to keep in mind that

> Poor people who respond to the evangelizing ministries may not choose to unite with the particular congregation sponsoring the ministry. Sponsors need to be ready to celebrate involvement with any part of the Body of Christ.

> Congregations receiving poor people as new members can expect to find some of their norms and procedures challenged and in need of revision in order to embrace a more diverse membership. Accordingly, clergy and official board support of this study is essential at all points.[13]

For example, churches attracting new Hispanic or Asian members may want to say the Lord's Prayer in both English and the language of the new members. It is generally not a good idea to offer complete services in both languages, because this may tend to split the congregation permanently, rather than to integrate one group with the other. Music of different cultures can also be incorporated into the hymn singing or anthems. In addition, churches with new African-American members may want to include the spirituality and joy found in many black churches in their worship and song. Once such new members are part of the church, it is important to learn from their culture and tradition, and not just to incorporate them into ours, thereby denying the richness of cultural diversity.

An excellent workshop has been published by the United Methodist Church to prepare congregations for integrating new members of different cultures. *The Language of Hospitality: Intercultural Relations in the Household of God* contains six sessions designed to help a parish deal with the sensitive issues of race and culture in our society today. Offering such a workshop may be quite helpful to congregations as they reach out to members of different cultures.[14]

Church members who want to minister with the poor can receive advanced training. A superb training program, with leader's guide, is *Evangelism with the Poor* by the Rev. Ann Elizabeth Proctor McElligott, published by the Episcopal Church Center. The first five sessions of the program provide appropriate training and include an examination of participants' feelings regarding the poor, Old and New Testament perspectives, the participants' own values discussed in light of the values of the kingdom of God, and a format for discussing visits to existing community ministries with the poor.[15] For the sixth and seventh training sessions, the Listening Skills Workshop in Chapter 2 of this book can be used. Helping volunteers become good story-listeners is critical to ministry with the poor. Helping them listen for the word of God revealed to them through the poor is equally important for their own development as lay ministers.

In addition to initial training, lay ministers can be offered ongoing training, support, and reflection. At the beginning of each session, they might spend twenty minutes on listening skills training, using Exercise 4 from the second session of the Listening Skills Workshop found on pages 45-46. It is best to have participants provide their own "problem scenarios" for this exercise. This ministry can also raise numerous questions that may need to be dealt with from a spiritual perspective by a trained leader. A monthly co-workers' meeting, offering prayer, Bible study, time for reflection, and sharing of experiences, is most helpful in preventing volunteer burnout and in meeting the needs of those involved. At each meeting, attending to one's own spiritual needs can be discussed with co-workers. In Mother Teresa's clinic for lepers in Calcutta, India, the following Hindu poem hangs on the wall:

> If you have two pieces of bread,
> Give one to the poor,
> Sell the other,
> And buy hyacinths
> To feed your soul.[16]

This poem offers a much-needed reminder of the importance of self-care to those who minister in the name of Christ.

As we develop programs for reaching out to the poor in our own communities, it is important to keep one thought at the center of our hearts. As Henri Nouwen writes in *Reaching Out: Three Movements of the Spiritual Life*, this ministry of hospitality, like all others, "points to someone higher than our thoughts can reach, someone deeper than our hearts can feel and wider than our arms can embrace, someone under whose wings we can find refuge (Psalm 90) and in whose love we can rest, someone we call our God."[17]

A EUCHARIST IN REMEMBRANCE OF THE DEPARTED PRAYER, SCRIPTURE, AND HYMN SUGGESTIONS

Gather in the Lord's Name

Proclaim and Respond to the Word of God

Lesson from Hebrew Scripture
Ecclesiastes 3:1-8 (For everything there is a season)
Isaiah 40:28-31 (God gives power to the faint)
Isaiah 49:13-15 (The Lord will have compassion on those who suffer)
Wisdom 3:1-3,9 (The souls of the righteous are in the hand of God)

The Psalm
(After the lesson from Hebrew scripture, "A Psalm About Grieving," found on page 113 may be used, or one of the following Psalms may be sung or said:)

Psalm 18, Part I	Psalm 102
Psalm 23	Psalm 121
Psalm 42	Psalm 139

The Gospel
Matthew 26:36-46 (Jesus prays in the Garden of Gethsemane)
John 11:21-27 (I am the resurrection and the life)
John 14:1-6 (In my Father's house are many mansions)
John 20:11-18 (Jesus appears to Mary outside the tomb)

The Homily

Offer Prayers
Collects—Prayers of the Day
  O Comforting One, Compassionate One, be with us all when we suffer loss, and ache with the pain of grieving. Give us a glimpse of the way it will be when love will never be taken away, when life itself will not be diminished, when all that we hold most precious will live and remain with us forever. Amen.

WOMANWISDOM: A *Feminist Lectionary and Psalter—Women of the Hebrew Scriptures: Part One,* Miriam Therese Winter, New York, Crossroad Publishing Company, © 1991, 250. Reprinted by permission.

  Most merciful God, whose wisdom is beyond our understanding: Deal graciously with your people in their grief. Surround them with your love, that they may not be overwhelmed by their loss, but have confidence in your goodness, and strength to meet the days to come; through Jesus Christ our Lord. Amen.

The Book of Common Prayer, New York, The Church Hymnal Corporation, 1979, 494.

  Eternal Lord God, you hold all souls in life: Give to your whole Church in paradise and on earth your light and your peace; and grant that we, following the good examples of those who have served you here and are now at rest, may at the last enter with them into your unending joy; through Jesus Christ our Lord, who lives and reigns with you, in the unity of the Holy

Spirit, one God, now and for ever. Amen.

The Book of Common Prayer, New York, The Church Hymnal Corporation, 1979, 253.

God of love, we thank you for all with which you have blessed us even to this day: for the gift of joy in days of health and strength, and for the gifts of your abiding presence and promise in days of pain and grief. We praise you for home and friends, and for our baptism and place in your Church with all who have faithfully lived and died. Above all else we thank you for Jesus, who knew our griefs, who died our death and rose for our sake, and who lives and prays for us. Amen.

The Book of Services, Nashville, The United Methodist Publishing House, © 1985, 83. Reprinted by permission.

Almighty God, look with pity upon the sorrow of your servants, for whom we pray. Amidst things they cannot understand, help them to trust in your care. Bless them and keep them. Make your face to shine upon them and be gracious to them. Lift up your countenance upon them and give them peace. Amen.

The Book of Services, Nashville, The United Methodist Publishing House, © 1985, 90. Reprinted by permission.

Prayers of the People

Leader: Come, let us praise our God of mercy and compassion.

People: Whose love is everlasting.

Leader: For helping us survive the loss of our loved one.

People: We thank you, God.

Leader: For forgiving, loving, and watching over all those we remember today and name at this time . . . We thank you, God.

Leader: For all those who helped us through the aftermath,

People: We thank you, God.

Leader: For the love and concern we share for one another, as members of the body of Christ,

People: We thank you, God.

Leader: Above all, we thank you for your child, our Savior,
          Jesus Christ; for our hope in him, for the joy of serving
          him, and for the promise of life everlasting with you.

Leader and People: O God, refuge of all who weep, we commend
          to you now our grief in the death of our loved ones,
          trusting in your compassion and mercy toward them.
          Surround us with your loving presence when feelings of
          guilt, anger, blame, or deep sorrow threaten to over-
          come us. Cast out our fear with your perfect love. Heal
          our wounds. Bind up our broken hearts. Protect us, as a
          mother bear protects her cubs. Lead us, as a tender
          shepherd leads his flock. All this we ask in the name of
          your child, our Savior Jesus Christ, who lived, and
          died, and lives again that we may know the joy of your
          resurrection. Amen.

Portions of the Prayers of the People were adapted from *After Suicide*, John
Hewett, Philadelphia, Westminster Press, 1980, 113-115. Closing prayer written by Elizabeth R. Geitz after the death of her mother.

Exchange the Peace
(If desired, there can be a Sharing of Memories by those who
wish to do so, immediately following the peace. This could be
used in place of a Homily.)

Prepare the Table

Celebrate the Eucharist

Sing Hymns
       There is a Balm in Gilead
       Amazing Grace
       O Master, Let Me Walk With Thee
       The Strife is O're
       For All the Saints, stanzas 1, 2, and 4.
       O God, Our Help in Ages Past
       Love Divine, All Loves Excelling

A PSALM ABOUT GRIEVING

Choir 1	I turned to the wind who howled and sighed the whole time I was healing.
Choir 2	I turned to a tree who had lost its leaves— she knew how I was feeling.
Choir 1	I turned to the rain who was in tears, for I too felt like crying.
Choir 2	I turned to the earth who understood what it meant to live with dying.
Choir 1	I turned to a thistle in a field, I could see she too was lonely.
Choir 2	I turned to a rock who knew how hard it was to be one and only.
Choir 1	I turned to a blade of grass because there were bonds I had to sever.
Choir 2	I turned to the sea who returned to me and taught me about forever.
Choir 1	I turned to a mountain who seemed secure and I asked for strength and endurance.
Choir 2	I turned to wildflowers in a wood and they gave me some assurance.
Choir 1	I turned to a friend who sat with me until she had to be leaving.
Choir 2	I turned to Shaddai Who stayed with me and helped me through my grieving.

BEREAVEMENT FOLLOW-UP[18]

Name(s) _____

Address _____

Phone_____ Clergy _____

Relationship to the deceased _____

Name and age of deceased _____

Date of death _____ Date of funeral _____

Funeral Director notified _____ Organist notified _____

Altar Guild notified_____ Worship participants notified_____

Burial Office planned _____ Program printed _____

DATE	TYPE OF VISIT	COMPLETED (Initial)
_____	One week after death	_____
_____	One month after death	_____
_____	Three months after death	_____
_____	Six months after death	_____
_____	One year anniversary of death	_____
_____	Two year anniversary of death	_____

(Staff will determine appropriate response on above dates.)

ADDITIONAL COMMENTS:

POEMS OF GRIEVING

EASTER MOURNING

The smell of lilies permeates my senses
As alleluias ring through the air.
"Rejoice. Christ is risen. Yes, risen indeed!"
Yet for me, I'm still on Golgotha.

Weeping, kneeling at the foot of the cross
Wounds bleeding, water flowing to mesh with my tears.
Ashes to ashes, dust to dust
But not now, not here, not this way!

"My God, my God, why have you forsaken me?"
O Wounded One, don't leave me, not now.
My pain is your pain and your pain is mine.
Flesh rips, hearts bleed, then it stops.

Now I'll carry you, as you've carried me
Giving birth to the you now within me.
Hearts mingle, tears spill as my love overflows
For the Wounded One, Risen One, live-giving Lover of Souls.

—Elizabeth Rankin Geitz

THE LIGHT

Blinded, exposed, we retreat
Secure in the dark that surrounds us.
One hand obscuring the source of all life
We hide, as if we're not seen.

Darkness beckons, cajoles, nurtures.
God's love, cocoon-like enfolds us.
Fetus floating, weightlessly, wondering
As Wisdom gradually seeps in.

Opening our fingers so slowly
We find that the light is still there.
Unchangeable, fathomless Mystery of Love
Creator creating anew.

—Elizabeth Rankin Geitz

HIDE-AND-SEEK

Enfold me, hold me, never let me go
O Silent One of the Fathomless Deep.
Tears flowing, heart seeking, feelings numbing
As pain overwhelms.

Where are you now in my long, dark night?
Hidden, teasing, you're here—then you're not.
Hide-and-seek? I'm too tired to play
As exhaustion sets in.

Yet seek you I must and seek you I will!
Oh, you're here? It was I who was hiding?
Come sit. I've been waiting all day.
Come sit. I have so much to say.

—Elizabeth Rankin Geitz

COMMUNITY NEEDS ASSESSMENT[19]
INTERVIEW FORM

Date _____

Interview with _____

Organization _____

Address _____

Telephone _____

1. How does the social service network in _____ handle emergencies?

2. Who asks you for help? How do you handle it?

3. What needs, normally met through social service agencies, are not currently being met here?

4. Do you know why the social service sector is not meeting these needs?

5. Are there any plans under way to establish an agency to meet these needs?

6. If a new ministry were established, what range of services would you like to see it provide?

7. What are the funding sources in this community for establishing such an outreach?

8. Who currently administers emergency funds in this community?

9. How are utility funds administered?

10. Ideally, how would you see area churches, synagogues, and other religious organizations participating in this venture?

11. What do you see as potential problem areas that might arise in (a) establishing this ministry, (b) running it?

12. Any other comments?

13. Who else do you recommend we interview?

Chapter 7

OUTREACH TO THE BUSINESS COMMUNITY

While working at Martin House, a Catholic settlement house in inner-city Trenton, New Jersey, I also attended various business functions with my husband, in my role as corporate wife. Going from an environment where people literally did not have enough to eat, into an elegant French restaurant in New York City, left me with much to think about. Being in the midst of such extremes of wealth and poverty in our country gnawed at my conscience, as well as my stomach, as I tried to eat the food. For what could be more destitute than an impoverished inner-city area faced with the social program cutbacks that characterized the 1980s? And what was more opulent than Wall Street in that same decade? Yet here I was regularly moving between these two separate and diverse worlds.

It sometimes happened that as a waiter presented me with an artistically arranged plate of food, my mind flashed back to the peanut butter sandwich I had made earlier for a student who had run out of food stamps on the twentieth of the month. I heard my sisters and brothers in the inner city crying out to me to do something, say *something* to the people around me, who had both the wealth and the power to make a difference. But what? I was clear that God was calling me to be in both of these settings. But why? What did God want *me* to do?

For a while I wallowed in guilt. I guess I thought that was the least I could do. But I soon realized that my guilt was helping no one, and I decided that there is no grace in guilt. Then came anger. Why did God have me in this situation? I did not like feeling this uncomfortable! But these feelings did not change anything either, so I continued to struggle.

I gradually accepted the fact that perhaps God had something to teach me and maybe I should just listen. Since making that decision more than seven years ago, I have been amazed at the consistent opportunity for ministry within a business environment. By merely mentioning my own involvement in a meaningful lay ministry, I found that the conversation would suddenly change from the superficial to the serious. For example, one person related concern over an employee who had had a male to female sex-change operation, which upset the women in his office to the extent that they refused to allow the individual to use the women's restroom. Another spoke of sleepless nights spent in worrying about people she had been told by her boss to fire, knowing that she might be next. Another voiced concern over whether to report on a co-worker who was using company funds illegally.

As I continued to listen, I found that there were numerous opportunities to ask a gentle question to prod someone's thinking along the lines of Christian values. Among the subjects people raised with me were homelessness, the housing problem, extremes of wealth and poverty in our country, the Gulf War, parenting concerns, and even prayer. I began to think of myself as Ms. Johnny Appleseed, planting seeds that could either grow and blossom or lie fallow. In most cases, I still do not know which happened. Yet it became clear to me that here was an opportunity to reach out to others in the name of Christ. If these people had not lived so far away from me, it would also have been quite natural to invite them to my church, particularly if there was a topic being discussed of interest to the business community.

Meanwhile, I still heard the cries of my sisters and brothers in the inner city, whose lives were often changed dramatically by economic decisions beyond their control. For example, many of them had been living in poverty since numerous factories in the Trenton area had either moved or had been closed. Others struggled to make high rent payments, because no banks would risk giving them a loan. Some were fired from their jobs when, under the law, the company would have had to start paying them benefits. Others were forced to stay on welfare because the jobs they could obtain did not offer any medical benefits. There was a strong link between these two diverse worlds, a link that cried out to be addressed.

I began to wonder if there might be some way that the institutional church could train countless Ms. and Mr. Johnny Appleseeds to be the hands and feet of Christ in the marketplace. For I believe that if the church is concerned about ministry with the poor, it should be equally concerned about ministry with those in positions of power, whose decisions affect the poor. Such a dual focus could do more to bring about change within systems than a single concentration on one group or the other.

Yet, where to begin? The task seemed insurmountable, for when I went from the church, where daily reminders of the sacred abound, into my husband's Wall Street office of marble, glass, and steel with no such reminders, I was overpowered by the contrast. The world of business to the outsider can seem to personify an ethos of competition, power, rugged individualism, and a focus on the bottom line, rather than on people. Can the gospel message somehow penetrate the marble and steel?

In today's business environment, where *hospitality* refers to the "hospitality suite" where customers are pursued, is there hope of a positive connection? In an environment where prophets are those who can successfully predict the rise and fall of the stock market, are Isaiah, Jeremiah, and Amos obsolete?

Let us hope not, for the decisions made by the leaders of business today affect the lives of thousands of workers and their families. Plant closings, corporate mergers, and major changes in corporate policy are decisions with far-reaching effects.

I decided to begin researching possible ways that the institutional church might reach out to those in the business community. The result of that research is what the rest of this chapter is about. What I am offering here is a proposal for a systematic outreach to the business community based on innovative parish programming and a responsiveness to pastoral needs. These suggestions are made in the hope that they might stimulate discussion within parishes and among churches on ways to reach out to the many business women and men in our midst. For I believe that nothing less than fulfilling a part of the gospel message in our time, is dependent upon such outreach.

In beginning my own journey of exploration of this issue, I began where I usually do, with the Bible. Was there any biblical basis for individuals to reach out to those in their professions in the name of Christ? Or would such outreach fall under the more general command of Jesus to "go therefore and make disciples of all nations" (Mt 28:19)? I was delighted to find that there is a powerful precedent for such mission, revealed to us through the life of Paul.

"After this Paul left Athens and went to Corinth. There he found a Jew named Aquila, a native of Pontus, who had recently come from Italy with his wife Priscilla, because Claudius had ordered all Jews to leave Rome. Paul went to see them, and, *because he was of the same trade*, he stayed with them, and they worked together—by trade they were tentmakers" (Acts 18:1–3 [Italics added]). Paul used his own profession as a tentmaker to establish a relationship with two other tentmakers, Aquila and Priscilla. In working together initially at their trade, these three tentmakers forged a missionary partnership that was far-reaching. Without this common bond of related work, who knows whether Paul would have been as successful in his missionary work with them?

Similarly, people in related areas of work can become successful missioners to one another today. To accomplish this task, I am proposing a twofold approach. First, after using the Hospitality Ministry Workshop (in Chapter 5), a congregation could offer the Hospitality in the Workplace Workshop (at the end of this chapter). *A natural move from a focus on hospitality within the church is to focus on hospitality within one's daily work environment.* The workshop begins with a focus on story-listening in the workplace and moves to inviting co-workers to church. It should be stressed that in engaging in such mission, laity need to refrain from using theological language and simply engage in story-listening. To meet people where they are requires listening to them, to see where God is already working in their lives. The Board for Social Responsibility of the Church of England writes that the task is not "to take Christ into the world of industry but to go there in order to find Him where He has gone ahead."[1] What a different focus this is! As laity go into the workplace, to find where Christ already is, they may be surprised at how often they encounter him.

For a number of years, the Church of England has been involved in industrial mission work. In an appraisal of that work, its Board for Social Responsibility has written, "The discovery of Jesus already present within the work setting and within the working out of economic and social issues is to be hoped for, and a Church which is not engaged in that discovery . . . is not evangelizing, because it is leaving aspects of human life and concern out of account."[2]

Jesus himself did not spend most of his time in the Temple or sanctuary. Instead, he was often found in the fields, by the lake, in the marketplace, with the fishermen and business people of his time. In Graham Tucker's *The Faith-Work Connection* he writes: "His stories and parables were designed to teach the values of the kingdom as they applied in everyday life and work. We are called to continue that ministry."[3]

To continue that ministry today requires not only parishioners who are interested in hospitality ministry in their workplace. It also requires that churches offer programs related to people's lives Monday through Friday, to attract those business persons in one's community who are lapsed church members or are unchurched. This brings us to the second phase of our approach to this outreach ministry.

The next step is for churches to offer specific forums and Bible study geared to meet the needs of those in the workplace. Why is this important? Because it may be easier for some parishioners to invite a co-worker to a Sunday morning series such as Ethics in the Workplace, than to simply invite that person to a worship service.

Several excellent resources are available for churches that wish to reach out to members of the business community. The Rev. John C. Haughey, S.J., a Jesuit priest, has written *Converting Nine to Five: A Spirituality of Daily Work*. Before writing this book, Haughey engaged people in reflection on the subject of work at seminars throughout the country: in Chicago at the Center for Ethics and Corporate Policy, in Kansas City at the Heartlands Conference, in Charlotte, North Carolina, with Charlotte's Executive Forum and Business Guild, in New York at the Wall Street Round Table on Ethics, and at Kirkridge, a retreat center in Bangor, Pennsylvania. His book contains an excellent study guide for churches to use in a chapter-by-chapter study. Chapter titles are "Meaning and Work," "The Creator God and Working People," "Work and Rest," "The God Who Works," "Evil at Work," "What Work Lasts?," "The Meaning God Sees," "A Spirituality of Work," and "A Method."[4]

Grace: God's Work Ethic by Paul G. Johnson, a Lutheran pastor, offers another resource for use on the parish level. His book "is a call for action that suggests how ministers and lay persons can help the church become a natural place for making the connections between the Gospel and weekday work. Included are practical ideas for developing support groups with both employed and unemployed workers, promoting dialogue between pastor and congregation, and reinforcing the new reformation in the workplace. For study groups, each chapter ends with conversation starter thoughts."[5]

The Alban Institute offers a creative workshop, *Linking Faith and Daily Life*. It contains six sessions entitled "Faith in the Workplace?," "Daily Life and Faith in My Situation," "My Family (or Primary Community) and My Work," "Working in Our Communities," "Everyone a Prophet," and "What Difference Can the Church Make?" Both a leader's guide and participant packet are included in this workshop that was sponsored by Auburn Theological Seminary and funded by Trinity Church in New York City.[6]

A comprehensive parish workshop, Ethics in the Workplace, can be found in *The Faith-Work Connection*, by Graham Tucker. Six different case studies are presented in his book, with questions for discussion and appropriate scripture quotations, the following cases are presented: Office Morale and Strife, Overtime and Personal Priorities, A Bad Work Environment–Stay or Quit?, Labour-Management Conflict, Technology Versus People, and Over the Hump.[7]

For such offerings to attract new members, they need to be advertised in the local newspaper and on the radio. Moreover, parishioners can be encouraged to bring a co-worker along with them. To increase the comfort level of parishioners who may not be used to inviting co-workers to church, the Hospitality in the Workplace Workshop at the end of this chapter may be offered first.

In addition to these Sunday morning programs, churches might want to consider offering Bible study during lunchtime in or near different workplaces in the community. Participants could bring their own lunches and study the lectionary reading for the following Sunday, a specific book of the Bible, or readings on a theme such as forgiveness. Such sessions may be led by the clergy or trained laypeople.

A business persons' breakfast and Bible study could also be offered on a weekday morning. This familiar method of reaching those within the business community has withstood the test of time and has proven to be successful in attracting new members to church.

Moreover, churches can offer a morning or noon-time gathering in which business women and men discuss issues within their workplace, as those issues relate to their lives as Christians. Such gatherings can foster a deep level of communication on particular issues of concern within the workplace.

An alternative to the study group, discussion group, and workshop methods is for churches to offer a large forum on Sunday morning that focuses on the connection between business and the church. To my delight, my research turned up some very tangible, nuts-and-bolts connections between the two. The material that follows on pages 125-129 (up to the paragraph beginning with "Servant leadership") can be presented at such a forum, which might also be advertised in the local newspaper and on the radio. The title of the forum could be "The Business-Church Connection."

More than six decades ago, the premier issue of *Business Week* magazine, dated September 7, 1929, included an article on the beginning of business. It stated: "It seems that business really began with the tolling of bells! In his latest book, *The Golden Age*, Lewis Mumford advances a curious theory as to the reason for the break-down of medieval culture and the dawn of the commercial era. . . . 'The first hint of change came in the thirteenth century with the ringing of the bells,' he says."[8] The ringing of church bells began to record the passing hour. People started to notice the succession of minutes and planned to make what they could of them. This innocent enjoyment of the regular tolling of the hour had important consequences. "Study modern business closely and you will find that it is built largely on materials, muscle, and minutes, and that minutes are today the controlling factor."[9]

It is indeed a curious theory that the church in some way begat the era of commercialism; yet this is the theory espoused by *Business Week* in its founding issue. Is this where the connection between the church and business begins and ends?

One American businessman in the 1920s was so distraught over the lack of connection he felt with the man called Jesus that he wrote about Jesus as the founder of modern business. In *The Man Nobody Knows*, Bruce Barton writes of Jesus as the ultimate executive, the outdoor man, the sociable man, the advertising man, and the founder of business. In his chapter called "The Executive," he writes, "Blazing conviction was the first and greatest element in the success of Jesus. The second was his wonderful power to pick men, and to recognize hidden capacities in them. . . . Nowhere is there such a startling example of executive success as the way in which that organization was brought together. . . . Having gathered together his organization, there remained for Jesus the tremendous task of training it. And herein lay the third great element in his success—his vast unending patience. . . . He believed that the way to get faith out of men is to show that you have faith in them; and from the great principle of executive management he never wavered."[10] This connection may seem comical at first, but it poignantly reveals both an underlying need for identification and an underlying truth about the connection between business and Christianity. Both at their hearts are people oriented. A good business takes care of its people. A good business is there to serve its community.

The move from the concept of business as a battleground to business as a place of service is captured in the following poem by Berton Braley:

Business Is Business[11]

"Business is Business," the Little Man said,
"A battle where 'everything goes,'
Where the only gospel is 'get ahead,'
And never spare friends or foes.
'Slay or be slain,' is the slogan cold;
You must struggle and slash and tear,
For Business is Business, a fight for gold,
Where all that you do is fair!"

"Business is Business," the Big Man said,
"A battle to make of earth
A place to yield us more clothes and bread,
More pleasure and joy and mirth;
There are still some bandits and buccaneers
Who are jungle-bred beasts of trade,
But their number dwindles with passing years
And dead is the code they made!"

"Business is Business," the Big Man said,
"But it's something that's more, far more;
For it makes sweet gardens of deserts dead,
And cities it built now roar
Where once the deer and gray wolf ran
From the pioneer's swift advance;
Business is Magic that toils for man,
Business is True Romance.

"And those who make it a ruthless fight
Have only themselves to blame
If they feel no whit of the keen delight
In playing the Bigger Game,
The game that calls on the heart and head,
The best of man's strength and nerve;
'Business is Business' " the Big Man said,
"And that Business is to serve!"

In the words of this simple poem, numerous business friends I have shared it with have seen themselves and have been able to laugh. Often against their will, they find themselves caught in a battle where indeed "the only gospel is 'get ahead.' " I believe it is the role of the church to help them move from the first stanza of this poem to the last.

In his landmark book, *Servant Leadership*, Robert K. Greenleaf, a Quaker and former Director of Management Research for AT&T, writes of businesses becoming service oriented through a model of servant leadership. "Perhaps I reflect the influence of my own vocational choice when I say that, in the next few years, more will be learned in business than in any other field about how to bring servant leadership into being as a major social force. In my view . . . businesses are more questioning of their own adequacy [than other institutions], they are more open to innovation, and they are disposed to take great risks to find a better way."[12] Greenleaf's prediction, written in 1970, did in fact bear fruit in the 1980s.

For instance, his prediction is borne out in *Communicating for Productivity*, a handbook outlining effective management techniques written by Roger D'Aprix in 1982. He advocates a "new" management style for business by outlining the views of the Rev.

Thomas McGrath, S.J., a priest, psychologist, and management consultant. McGrath points out that the events of the 1960s destroyed several automatic responses of the worker of the 1950s to institutional organizations. A solution to the reality of changed worker attitudes, he feels, is to begin to manage people through effective relationships. D'Aprix writes, "We must manage through respect for human dignity and human worth. What's more, he [McGrath] uses the love relationship as a model for what we need, to learn how to manage people more effectively."[13]

Sound familiar? Nothing is more fundamental to the Judeo-Christian tradition than the dignity of every human being, because that person is made in the image of God. "So God created humankind in his image, in the image of God he created them; male and female he created them. . . . God saw everything that he had made, and indeed, it was very good" (Gn 1:27, 31). It is for this reason that we are to love our neighbors as ourselves, putting this love relationship at the center of our lives as Christian people.

To put this maxim into practical application, McGrath makes four recommendations, one of which is directly in line with Greenleaf's proposal. First, he feels that managers must tell their people that they and their work are valuable. Second, the new manager must be prepared to give service to others. "This in no way diminishes the role or status of the manager. It merely changes it."[14] Third, the new manager will have to learn to give attention to the individual needs of people in her or his organization. Fourth, effective managers must learn to say "I'm sorry" when they have made a mistake.[15]

In their book *In Search of Excellence*, Thomas Peters and Robert Waterman also stress the importance of relationship. They advise managers to treat those who work for them "as partners; treat them with dignity; treat them with respect. . . . There was hardly a more pervasive theme in the excellent companies than *respect for the individual* (italics added)."[16] The book goes on to state that at J.C. Penney, people are referred to as "associates," not employees, and they are each listened to.[17] The authors cite numerous other examples of the importance of this business philosophy.

In theological language, this concept is called "authority as partnership" rather than "authority as domination." Feminist theologians such as Letty Russell have been advocating this model of relationship for a number of years. It is when we view everyone as an equal partner with us that we are applying long-held biblical traditions to our lives. These time-honored traditions make good business sense as well, as outlined in these books.

Servant leadership is an in-depth concept that merits more than an introductory forum. At the end of the forum, participants might be encouraged to attend a seminar on servant leadership. The Church of the Saviour in Washington, D.C., offers a Servant Leadership School with workshops scheduled year round.[18] In addition, the Kanuga Conference Center in Hendersonville, North Carolina, offers an Institute for Servant Leadership with workshops geared specifically for either clergy or lay leaders. The workshop was developed and is led by Episcopal Bishop Bennett Sims.[19]

Still another way of reaching out to the business community is offered by General Theological Seminary in New York City. Every other month, the seminary hosts panel discussions on topics of interest to local business leaders, sending them personal invitations. One 1991 series, "The Moral Dimensions Forum," was held from 6:00 P.M. to 7:30 P.M. and was followed by a brief reception. A list of area restaurants was provided for the participants' use after the forum. The topics in this particular series were What Shapes the Shapers of the News?; Personal Ethics, Religious Convictions and Public Service; The Moral Implications of U.S. Policy in the Persian Gulf; and The Moral Implications of Extraordinary Medical Measures Taken to Sustain Life. For each forum there were four panelists, who included a member of the clergy and experts in the topic for the evening. In addition, the seminary hosts dinners for area business leaders, addressing topics such as Moral Teaching on the Economic Order, Christian Perspectives on Business Ethics, The Gap Which Exists Between the Organized Church and the Business World, and The Pope Affirms the "New Capitalism."

It would be an unusual church indeed that could offer such a series, yet the seminary's approach can offer guidelines for such forums on the local level. For instance, a church might offer a forum, led by a local merchant, on Christian perspectives on dealing with customers on a daily basis. The local vice-president of a bank could speak on ethical decisions that arise within his or her job. An economics professor from a local community college might speak on her or his area of expertise as it relates to policies that affect the poor in our country. The list is endless, and choices would be determined by the members of a given parish.

Another matter of great weight for the church is the problem of unemployment in our country. With more and more people being laid off in today's marketplace, the church has a responsibility to reach out to all those who suddenly find themselves in this situation. "In American culture one of the first questions we pose to one another is 'What do you do?' This is a code phrase that we all understand immediately. It means tell me what your work is, and I will know who you are, how valuable you are, and where you fit in society."[20] Such stress on identification and self-worth through one's work is an unfortunate reality in our culture today. Thus, those who find themselves without a job can find themselves without the identity and self-worth that it provides.

In 1983 the Kings-Bay Chaplaincy in Toronto, Ontario, started Operation Bootstrap to respond to the unemployment crisis in the area. In the first four years of its existence, the group helped 1,300 people find or create new jobs for themselves. The program, open to people of all backgrounds and faiths, is based on sound spiritual values and principles; yet theological language is not used. Even so, one program participant wrote in the evaluation, "This has been the finest example of applied Christianity I have ever experienced."[22]

For clergy who would like to focus on the pastoral issues faced by people in the workforce or those who are unemployed, *In and Out of Work: A Pastoral Perspective*, by Paul H. Ballard, 1987, is a helpful resource. It is part of the series "Pastoral Care and Ethical Issues" published by the Saint Andrew Press in Edinburgh, Scotland.

When churches meet the pastoral needs of those in the workplace, they are responding to a major segment of their parishioners' lives. When they offer educational opportunities, enabling participants to see the connection between their faith and their work, they are offering an invaluable service both to their parishioners and to the communities they are there to serve. When they take the next step and train parishioners to reach out intentionally to their co-workers, offering them a place in the body of Christ, they are participating in a ministry that has the potential to be life changing, not only for those within the work environment, but for those whose lives are affected by the decisions they make.

In 1 Corinthians, Paul says, "For the kingdom of God depends not on talk but on power" (1 Cor 4:20). When the institutional church intentionally reaches out to those in positions of power, this effort can bring us one small step closer to the kingdom as God intended it to be. Reinhold Niebuhr speaks of such attempts to bring about the kingdom on earth as the impossible possibility. He writes that the "Kingdom of God is always a possibility in history because its heights of pure love are organically related to the experience of love in all human life, but it is also an impossibility in history and always beyond every historical achievement."[22]

Those churches that strive to live out this impossible possibility through actively reaching out to both the power*less* and the power*ful* may find themselves enriched beyond their own imaginings. For it is in reaching out to the many angels God sends our way that we receive the gifts they bring with them for us. It is in exploring, risking, and daring to take new steps that we move one small step closer to fulfilling the gospel mandate in our time.

Hospitality in the Workplace Workshop
Session 1

Materials Needed: Newsprint and marker

Quotation: "The task is not to take Christ into the workplace, but to go there in order to find him where he has gone ahead."

The Board for Social Responsibility,
the Church of England

1. Write the quotation above on newsprint for people to see as they enter the room. Begin the session by reading Acts 18:1–3 aloud. Point out that in this instance, Paul deliberately sought out people in his own profession to bring into the body of Christ. It was possibly this commonality that provided him with a basis on which he could build a deeper relationship. As a result, he ended up forging a missionary partnership with them that was far-reaching.

How can we become successful missioners with those in our

trade or profession? First, we can be clear about what our task is and what it is not. Read the quotation for this session aloud.

2. How do we go about meeting Christ in the workplace? First of all by listening to others. Read the following quotation by Taylor Caldwell aloud: "The most desperate need of people today is . . . not a new religion, or a new 'way of life.' . . . A people's real need, their most terrible need, is for someone to listen to them, not as a 'patient,' but as a human soul. They need to tell someone of what they think, of the bewilderment they encounter when they try to discover why they were born, how they must live, and where their destiny lies."[23] It is only by listening to others that we can learn where they are on their own faith journeys. It is only by listening that we will be able to discern when a simple question may help someone to begin thinking along the lines of Christian values.

3. Tell the story of one person's experience of story-listening within a business environment, found on page 120. Then ask, "Has God presented you with similar opportunities for ministry? What were they?" Give participants some time to reflect on this question. Then give them ten minutes to share their experience with one other person. Next, have them tell their experiences, or lack of experience, to the group as a whole.

4. Ask group members how they would feel about using such opportunities for lay ministry within the workplace. What do they feel would be most difficult? What would be easiest? Solicit answers from the group as a whole, then write their responses on newsprint.

Ask workshop participants to be on the lookout for opportunities for hospitality ministry in their workplace over the next week. Ask them to be prepared to share their experiences with the group in the next session, which should be scheduled one week later.

Session 2

Materials Needed:	Newsprint and marker, 3- by 5-inch cards and a pen for each participant
Quotation:	"The discovery of Jesus already present within the work setting and within the working out of economic and social issues is to be hoped for, and a Church which is not engaged in that discovery . . . is not evangelizing, because it is leaving aspects of human life and concern out of account."

The Board for Social Responsibility,
the Church of England

1. Write the quotation above on newsprint for all to see as they enter the room. Begin this session by reading the quotation aloud. Stress again that the task is not to bring Christ into the workplace, but to discover where he is already there in our midst.

2. Next, ask participants to relate one opportunity for hospitality ministry in the workplace that they encountered during the last week, to one other person in the group. Then, have them share their experiences with the group as a whole. Allow plenty of time to address participants' feelings about their opportunities.

3. Discuss inviting co-workers to church. State that research has shown that three out of four previously unchurched persons were influenced by a friend or family member to come to church. The body of Christ grows person by person, family by family, through a lay person who cares enough about a friend or colleague to offer that person a bridge to relationship with Christ and his church. If the invitation does not begin with loving concern it will not succeed. It is important to stress that the invitation is always God's, not ours or our church's.[24]

Give each person a 3- by 5-inch card and have participants write down the names of co-workers who are unchurched whom they would feel comfortable inviting to church. Then ask them to pray for those people every day for the next two weeks.

Urge members of the group, after continuing to engage in story-listening in their workplaces and continuing to pray for specific individuals, to invite these people to attend one of the special forums for the business community that your church plans to offer.

NOTES

Chapter 1

1. John Koenig, *New Testament Hospitality: Partnership with Strangers as Promise and Mission* (Philadelphia: Fortress Press, 1985), 15, 46. I highly recommend this book for a thorough, in-depth discussion of hospitality in the New Testament.

2. Ibid., 16. This information is taken from Amos 9:13–15; Joel 3:18; and early extra-biblical Jewish literature—the Testament of Levi 18:11, 1 Enoch 62:14, and Midrash Exodus 25:7–8.

3. Ibid., 17.

4. Ibid.

5. James M. Brice, author, Rebel C. Forrester and Betty B. Wood, ed., *I Had a Real Good Time: The Making of a Country Editor* (Union City, Tennessee: Forrester and Wood Publ., 1984), 59.

6. *The Book of Common Prayer* (New York: The Church Hymnal Corp., 1979), 305. This is taken from the rite of Holy Baptism used by the Episcopal Church. Other denominations use similar wording.

7. Mary Sammons Patton, *Hearts Birds Freed: Collected Essays in Verse* (Princeton, New Jersey, The Patton Family, 1992), 98–99.

8. Leonard Swidler, *Biblical Affirmations of Woman* (Philadelphia: Westminster Press, 1979), 183–185.

9. Ibid., 189.

10. Koenig, *New Testament Hospitality*, 99.

11. Ibid.

135

12. Patton, *Hearts Birds Freed*, 13.

13. Howard W. Stone, *The Word of God and Pastoral Care* (Nashville: Abingdon Press, 1988), 56.

14. Ibid., 57.

15. Margaret Guenther, *Holy Listening: The Art of Spiritual Direction* (Boston: Cowley Publications, 1992), 10.

16. Stone, *The Word of God*, 70.

17. Henri Nouwen, *Reaching Out: The Three Movements of the Spiritual Life* (New York: Doubleday & Co., 1975), 86.

18. Guenther, *Holy Listening*, 11–12.

19. Koenig, *New Testament Hospitality*, 8.

Chapter 2

1. Taylor Caldwell, *The Listener* (New York: Doubleday & Co., 1960), Introduction. The language in this quotation has been changed to be more inclusive.

2. Geoffrey Chaucer, *The Canterbury Tales* (Great Britain: Harper Collins, 1964), 25–26. This text has been rendered in modern prose by David Wright.

3. Gloria Durka, *Praying with Julian of Norwich* (Winona, Minnesota: St. Mary's Press, 1989), 13.

4. Henri J.M. Nouwen, *Reaching Out: The Three Movements of the Spiritual Life* (New York: Doubleday & Co., 1975), 74.

5. Ibid., 77.

6. Wayne Schwab and William A. Yon, *Proclamation As Offering: Story and Choice* (New York: Episcopal Church Center, 1988), 27.

7. David Grossman, *The Yellow Wind* (New York: Farrar, Straus and Giroux, 1988), 67. Translated from the Hebrew by Haim Watzman.

8. Henry Ralph Carse, a private communication; from his forthcoming book.

9. The Listening Skills Workshop offered at the end of this chapter is designed to provide an introduction to the concept of story-listening and mutual listening for the word of God. However, it takes much more than one workshop for people to

acquire this skill. With this in mind, for further training in active listening skills, I recommend that laypersons call the local CONTACT helpline in their area. CONTACT is an international organization, accessible in most areas of the United States, that was begun by a minister in Australia. Its 52-week training program for telephone hotline workers offers the best active listening skills training for lay people that I have found anywhere. In addition, information is provided on helping people with a variety of problems. Those who sign up for this course should be prepared to work on the telephone helpline, which provides additional practice in listening skills.

10. Thomas Gordon, *Parent Effectiveness Training* (New York: Peter H. Wyden, Inc., 1970), 40–41. This exercise has been adapted from a similar exercise in Gordon's book.

11. Caldwell, *The Listener*, Introduction.

12. Nouwen, *Reaching Out*, 86.

13. Ibid.

14. John Koenig, *New Testament Hospitality: Partners with Strangers as Promise and Mission* (Philadelphia: Fortress Press, 1985), 8.

15. Howard W. Stone, *The Word of God and Pastoral Care* (Nashville: Abingdon Press, 1988), 70.

Chapter 3

1. Arlin J. Rothauge, *Sizing Up a Congregation for New Member Ministry* (New York: Episcopal Church Center), 5.

2. Ibid., 19.

3. Michael K. Deaver with Mickey Herskowitz, *Behind the Scenes* (New York: William Morrow and Co., Inc., 1987), 82-83. This excerpt is reprinted with permission. I initially read this material in Howard Hanchey, *Church Growth and the Power of Evangelism: Ideas That Work* (Boston: Cowley Publications, 1990), 113–114.

4. St. Columba's Episcopal Church, Washington, D.C., Sunday bulletin, July 12, 1992.

5. Herb Miller, *How to Build a Magnetic Church* (Nashville: Abingdon Press, 1987), 67.

6. Ibid., 72–73.

7. Ibid., 73.

8. Hanchey, *Church Growth and the Power of Evangelism*, 150.

9. This paragraph is taken from my article, "How to Make Your Newcomer Program More Effective," *Action Information* (January, February 1986). *Action Information* is a publication of the Alban Institute, Washington, D.C.

10. This and the four paragraphs that precede it are adapted from the article mentioned above, "How to Make Your Newcomer Program More Effective."

11. Unpublished material taken from All Saints Church Covenant Program (Winter 1992). All Saints is located in Pasadena, California.

12. This quotation and the following information on family and pastoral size congregations are taken from an interview with the Rev. Alice B. Mann, author of *Incorporation of New Members in the Episcopal Church: A Manual for Clergy and Lay Leaders* (New York: Ascension Press, 1983).

13. John Koenig, *New Testament Hospitality: Partnership With Strangers as Promise and Mission* (Philadelphia: Fortress Press, 1985), 145.

Chapter 5

1. Taylor Caldwell, *The Listener* (New York: Doubleday and Co., 1960), Introduction. The language in this quotation has been changed to be more inclusive.

2. Roy M. Oswald, "Incorporating New Members into Parish Life," *Ministry Development Journal* (Spring 1984), 9.

3. Robert Gribbon, *When People Seek the Church* (Washington D.C.: Alban Institute, 1982), 11.

4. Ibid., 5, 12.

5. Ibid., 17.

6. Christopher Chamberlin Moore, Director of Communication, Episcopal Diocese of New Jersey. Chris is also the author of an excellent book, *What I Really Want to Do: How to Discover the Right Job*, published by Chalice Press.

7. Herb Miller, *How to Build a Magnetic Church* (Nashville: Abingdon Press, 1987), 31.

8. Alice Mann, *Incorporation of New Members in the Episcopal Church: A Manual for Clergy and Lay Leaders* (New York: Ascension Press, 1983), 21.

9. Miller, *How to Build a Magnetic Church*, 40.

10. Mann, *Incorporation of New Members*, 7.

11. Miller, *How to Build a Magnetic Church*, 35–36.

12. Mann, 30.

13. William Heuss, "The Last Pew," *The Episcopal Times*, Boston: Diocese of Massachusetts. This cartoon is printed here with the permission of the Rev. William Heuss.

14. The message on this Act of Friendship tablet was developed by the Newcomer Committee, Grace Church, Plainfield, New Jersey, during a presentation of this introductory workshop in 1987.

15. Miller, *How to Build a Magnetic Church*, 63. Reproduced by kind permission of the author.

16. The handout on covenant groups was developed by All Saints Church, Pasadena, California.

Chapter 6

1. "Study Holds Promise for Evangelism," *Episcopal Life* (August 1992), 16. The study, "Churches and Church Membership in the United States," is available from Glenmary Research Center, 750 Piedmont Avenue, Atlanta, Georgia 30308. The 456-page volume costs $36.

2. Frederick Houk Borsch, *Power in Weakness* (Philadelphia: Fortress Press, 1983), 125.

3. Robert McAfee Brown, *Unexpected News: Reading the Bible with Third World Eyes* (Philadelphia: Westminster Press, 1984), 99.

4. Ibid., 98–99.

5. Ibid., 67.

6. Ann Elizabeth Proctor McElligott, *Evangelism with the Poor: Leader's Guide* (New York: Episcopal Church Center, 1990), 6, 7.

7. Dominique Lapierre, *The City of Joy* (New York: Doubleday & Co., 1985), 40. Translated from the French by Kathryn Spinx.

8. Excerpt from Dr. Lupton's newsletter as quoted in McElligott, *Evangelism with the Poor*, 33. Used by permission.

9. Elizabeth R. Geitz for Grace Church, Plainfield, New Jersey, *On Loving Our Neighbors* (Plainfield, New Jersey: Wardens and Vestry of Grace Church, 1988), 14.

10. Thomas W. Ogletree, *Hospitality to the Stranger: Dimensions of Moral Understanding* (Philadelphia: Fortress Press, 1985), 3, 4.

11. Robert Gallagher, "Stay in the City," (Cincinnati: Forward Movement Publications, 1981), 36.

12. Ibid.

13. McElligott, *Evangelism with the Poor*, VI.

14. Anne Streaty Wimberly and Edward Powell Wimberly, *The Language of Hospitality: Intercultural Relations in the Household of God* (Nashville: Cokesbury). This book can be ordered by calling 1-800-672-1789.

15. McElligott, *Evangelism with the Poor*. This workshop can be ordered by calling Episcopal Parish Services, New York, at 1-800-223-2337.

16. Lapierre, *The City of Joy*, 233.

17. Henri J.M. Nouwen, *Reaching Out: The Three Movements of the Spiritual Life* (New York: Doubleday & Co., 1975), 86.

18. Elizabeth R. Geitz, "Bereavement Follow-Up," for the Bereavement Group of Trinity Church, Princeton, New Jersey. Trinity prints this material on the front and back of cards and keeps them alphabetized in a file box.

19. Community Needs Assessment is from *On Loving Our Neighbors*, Elizabeth R. Geitz (Plainfield, New Jersey: Wardens and Vestry of Grace Church, 1988), 14.

Chapter 7

1. Board for Social Responsibility, The Church of England, *Industrial Mission: An Appraisal* (London: General Synod Board for Social Responsibility, 1988), 38.

2. Ibid., 48.

3. Graham Tucker, *The Faith-Work Connection* (Toronto: Anglican Book Centre, 1987), 44.

4. John C. Haughey, *Converting Nine to Five: A Spirituality of Daily Work* (New York: Crossroad Publishing, 1989), 7.

5. Paul G. Johnson, *Grace: God's Work Ethic—Making Connections Between the Gospel and Weekday Work* (Valley Forge: Judson Press, 1985).

6. Robert E. Reber, *Linking Faith and Daily Life: An Educational Program for Lay People* (Washington, D.C.: The Alban Institute, 1991). This workshop can be ordered by calling 1-800-457-2674.

7. Tucker, *The Faith-Work Connection*, 194–200.

8. Robert R. Updegraff, "Trend and Tempo," *Business Week* (7, September 1929), 52.

9. Ibid.

10. Bruce Barton, *The Man Nobody Knows* (Indianapolis: The Bobbs-Merrill Co., 1924), 23–28.

11. James Gilchrist Lawson, ed., *The World's Best-Loved Poems* (New York: Harper & Row, 1955), 22–23.

12. Robert K. Greenleaf, *Servant Leadership: A Journey into the Nature of Legitimate Power and Greatness* (New York: Paulist Press, 1977), 134.

13. Roger D'Aprix, *Communicating for Productivity* (New York: Harper & Row, 1982), 16.

14. Ibid., 17.

15. Ibid.

16. Thomas J. Peters and Robert H. Waterman, *In Search of Excellence: Lessons from America's Best-Run Companies* (New York: Harper & Row, 1982), 238.

17. Ibid., 246–247.

18. The Servant Leadership School is an expression of The Church of the Saviour, Washington, D.C. To receive information about course offerings, call 202-328-7312 or write The Festival Center, Servant Leadership School, 1640 Columbia Rd. N.W., Washington, D.C. 20009.

19. To obtain information about the Institute for Servant Leadership, write to Bishop Bennett Sims, P.O. Box 1081, Hendersonville, NC 28793.

20. D'Aprix, *Communicating for Productivity*, 15.

21. Tucker, *The Faith-Work Connection*, 140.

22. Reinhold Niebuhr, *An Interpretation of Christian Ethics* (San Francisco: Harper & Row, 1935), 19.

23. Taylor Caldwell, *The Listener* (New York: Doubleday & Co., 1960), Introduction. The language in this quotation has been changed to be more inclusive.

24. Alice Mann, *Incorporation of New Members in the Episcopal Church: A Manual for Clergy and Lay Leaders* (New York: Ascension Press, 1983), 7.